LIFE IN PREHISTORIC TIMES

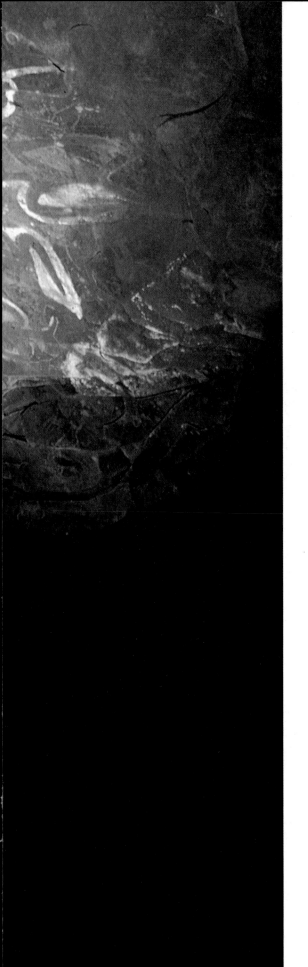

LIFE IN
PREHISTORIC
TIMES

Reader's
Digest

Published by
THE READER'S DIGEST ASSOCIATION LIMITED
London   New York   Sydney
Montreal   Cape Town

SNOW BLIND An inhabitant of the
Arctic made these 'sunglasses'
from caribou antler, to protect
against the glare of sun on snow.

EARLY HOMINID The skull of an
early human ancestor from East
Africa shows the links between
humankind and the apes.

LIFE IN PREHISTORIC TIMES
Edited and designed by Toucan Books Limited
Sole author: Linda Gamlin

First edition copyright © 1997
The Reader's Digest Association Limited
11 Westferry Circus, Canary Wharf, London E14 4HE

Reprinted 1999

Copyright © 1997
Reader's Digest Association Far East Limited
Philippines copyright © 1997
Reader's Digest Association Far East Limited

Printing and binding: Printer Industria Gráfica S.A.,
Barcelona
Separations: Rodney Howe Limited, London
Paper: Perigord-Condat, France

ISBN 0 276 42132 9

Front Cover (clockwise from top left): Sharpening a
needle using a flint; late Neolithic flint-bladed
dagger; activities at a copper mine; woolly mammoth;
cave painting of a warrior, Tassili N'Ajjer; ceramic
head symbolising life and death, Mexico; the head of
Tollund Man.

Back Cover (clockwise from top left): Caribou antler
'sunglasses', Thule culture, Arctic Canada;
Poulnabrone-Dolmen, Lisdonbarna, Ireland;
Neolithic pot from China; chess board from Mohenjo
Daro, Pakistan; knotted and plaited scabbard,
Neolithic; face of muzzled animal from feathered
headdress, Paracas style, Peru.

Page 1: A weary warrior returns to camp in a rock
painting from Tassili N'Ajjer in the Sahara.

Pages 2-3: Frigate birds were painted on the walls of
a cave on Easter Island more than 1000 years ago.

CONTENTS

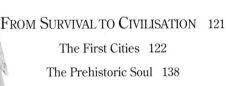

ANCIENT WEAPON A wooden-handled flint dagger and its sheath were preserved in a glacier in the European Alps.

OFFICIAL NAME An inscription from over 5000 years ago tells us that this Sumerian official was called Gudea.

STAYING SHARP A Peruvian flint blade, 11 000 years old, was wrapped in deer-hide to keep the blade sharp.

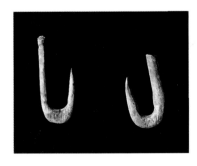

TO CATCH A FISH Hooks for line-fishing were carved from bone by people known as the Natufians who lived in the Near East 10 000 years ago.

AFTER LIFE This pottery urn, found in a burial mound in England, held the ashes of the dead.

THE DAWN OF MANKIND

Some 5 million years ago, as the tropical forests of Africa gave way to

encroaching grassland, our distant ancestors – it is thought – came down from the trees

and gradually adapted to life in the open country.

THEIR DAY BEGINS when the sun rises. The first glimmer of light wakes them, and they stretch and look at the horizon. Soon the cool, moist air of night-time starts to disperse and the fierce rays of the African sun begin to play upon their bodies. They are thirsty and, below them, the waters of the river glint invitingly. But they must be cautious. Before descending from their sleeping places in the trees they check carefully, scanning the surrounding plain and scrutinising the river bank for leopards or other predators. They call to one another; noises of reassurance or alarm, depending on what they observe below.

Perhaps they also speak a few rudimentary words, sounds that denote 'leopard' or 'lion', 'snake' or 'sabre-tooth tiger'. However, the shape of their larynx and their mouth is ape-like and does not allow them to articulate sounds with any great precision. They possess slightly larger brains than their immediate ape-like ancestors, and this increased intelligence gives them a more resourceful and imaginative approach to finding food, and a flair for solving practical problems.

When they are sure all is safe, they descend. Crouching on the river bank, they try to scoop up water in their hands to drink. But the dry season has begun, and the river level has fallen so far that the water is out of reach from the bank. They pick

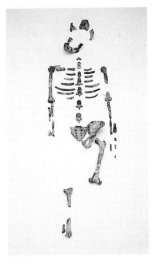

ANCIENT BONES
The skeleton of Lucy,
a female *Australopithecus
afarensis,* is over 3 million
years old.

long leathery leaves from nearby bushes which they use to dip into pools of water, each individual patiently drinking from a leaf, a few drops at a time. Heat and aridity are major problems for these hominids – distant members of the human family living in East Africa 3.5 million years ago, and known to modern science as *Australopithecus afarensis.* The climate which they endure is slowly drying out, as it has been now for several thousand years. Each year the forests of Africa die back a little farther, the outermost trees giving up the battle with the drought. Grass now grows where once there were forests, and the hominids, descendants of forest-dwelling apes, have made the crucial transition to savannah life. The key to their survival is finding food out on the plain.

Scattered across the open grassland are a few isolated trees that can withstand the drought; these include the tough, thorny acacias and the mighty baobabs with water stored in their swollen trunks. Along the river banks, many other trees continue to thrive, forming narrow ribbons of darker green vegetation – lush winding tracks of forest that dissect the dry sun-bleached savannah. It is in these riverside forests that the hominids take refuge. The coolness, the green light and damp, echoing air feel welcoming to them, for the forest is still in their blood. Ancient instincts bring them back here every night, or drive them on across the plains to another riverine forest strip.

High up in the trees, few predators can reach them, except for leopards. There is a powerful

DAWN OF HUMANKIND A group of early hominids
come down from the trees to drink at a river.
The hard facts about them, obtained from fossil bones,
must be fleshed out with informed guesswork.

sense of safety in the tree canopy, and they climb with enormous agility and skill. The long slender bones in their feet are slightly curved, moulding the foot around branches and giving a good grip. Using their long sinewy arms, they can support themselves by hanging below a large bough.

Down on the ground, they walk upright. Their legs are long, and they move with confident strides. It is this that separates them from the apes, their close relatives who still live in the remaining forests. Apes can rear up and take a few clumsy steps on their short hind legs, but most of the time they travel on all fours, folding their hands into fists and resting their weight on the knuckles.

Walking upright gives these hominids a far better view of the surrounding terrain and of any predators or potential threats. Rivers and lakes can be spied out more easily, and the group can keep together. Equally important, hominids are less directly exposed to the overhead midday sun by standing upright, since its rays encounter less body surface than if the hominids went on all fours.

Much of the hominids' day is probably occupied by the search for food. Before leaving the riverside, they eat any edible berries or nuts they can find there, and perhaps catch a frog or an insect. These foods are eaten immediately, with little preparation, other than cracking open the nuts, pulling the spiky legs off the insects, or perhaps rubbing the toxic spines from a fat caterpillar and wiping it clean with a leaf.

As soon as the resources of the strip of forest by the river are exhausted, the hominids move out onto the savannah, scavenging from the kills made by animals such as lions and tigers, and constantly scanning the horizon nervously for any sign of trouble. Some may take fallen branches or sticks with them, carrying them in their hands, to be waved threateningly if predators approach the group – another advantage of upright walking.

DANGEROUS RIVALS

At the first sign of danger – the approach of a hungry pride of lions, say – the hominids react with shrieks of alarm, and run to the nearest acacia tree. One hominid holds the leg of a scavenged antelope in his hand, and manages to climb the tree without dropping the carcass. The hominids are able to complete their meal aloft, while the lions circle about below.

Being able to carry food to places of safety is another benefit of being bipedal. They stay there once the meat is finished, and pass the hottest hours of the day in the acacia. The lions eventually become bored with waiting and wander off.

The chicks of ground-nesting birds, such as

EARTH'S BEGINNINGS AND TH

• About 4500 million years ago: the Earth was formed	• 3400-3300 million years ago: the oldest signs of life; evidence comes from rocks formed in Australia and South Africa	• 570-510 million years ago: animal forms, such as trilobites, developed	• 510-439 million years ago: the first fish appeared	• 439-409 million years ago: plants first invaded the land	• 363-290 million years ago: the first reptiles appeared	• 245 million years ago: there were mass extinctions	• 208-65 million years ago: dinosaurs dominated the Earth

• 50 000 years ago: First settlers in Australia	• 32 000 years ago: Earliest evidence for human settlement in the New World	• 12 500 years ago: Earliest pottery from Japan	• 10 000 BC: Earliest evidence for domesticated dog, from Natufian, Israel	• 10 000 BC: Early farming in the Fertile Crescent	• 7000 BC: Copper first used for making tools

TIMELINE Earth was already about 1000 million years old when the first forms of life began to emerge. Modern humans arrived

SITE OF DISCOVERY At Olduvai Gorge in East Africa, a river has sliced through the rock, revealing ancient fossils.

francolins and guinea fowl, are probably caught occasionally. Far more rewarding, however, are the giant eggs of ostriches. An unattended ostrich nest attracts other predators, such as baboons, but the hominids see off these competitors. The eggs are carried off before their custodian, the male ostrich, can return, since he is a ferocious enemy, quite capable of killing a hominid with one kick from his powerful clawed foot.

Carrying the eggs to a shady spot beneath a thorn tree, the hominids break them open by smashing the shells with a sharp stone. It takes skill to break an opening into the egg without shattering the shell completely, and thereby letting the

MAJOR EVENTS OF PREHISTORY

● 65 million years ago: the mass extinction of the dinosaurs took place and mammals appeared	● Over 3.7 million years ago: *Australopithecus afarensis*	● 2.5 million years ago: *Homo habilis*	● 1.8 million years ago: *Homo erectus*	● 200 000 years ago: Neanderthals	● 100 000 years ago: *Homo sapiens*

● 5200 BC: Neolithic Age in central and north-west Europe	● 3500 BC: Early city states in Mesopotamia	● 3300 BC: Pictographic signs on clay tablets from Uruk in Iraq were the precursors of cuneiform writing	3100 BC: Egyptian hieroglyphic writing was developed	2500 BC: Large urban centres such as Mohenjo Daro in the Indus Valley	2300 BC: European Bronze Age	800 BC: European Iron Age	AD 1000: New Zealand settled by Polynesian seafarers

about 100 000 years ago; major developments in their story are charted in the orange-coloured band.

FOOTPRINTS IN THE ASHES This trail of footprints in Tanzania was left in a layer of volcanic ash that had been turned to mud by the rain. Two adults and a child walked here more than 3 million years ago.

contents run out onto the ground. The first egg they open is wasted in this way but they get better with practice, until finally they can make an opening of exactly the right size for scooping out the liquid contents of the egg.

Practising, experimenting, improving new-found skills – these are key attributes of the hominids, a sign of their developing intelligence. While the others dip into ostrich eggs with their hands, perhaps there is one hominid who examines a curved fragment of shell thoughtfully. With the next egg, she tries using the broken piece to dip into the egg and spoon out the nutritious liquid. She is successful in this, and when they leave she carries the piece of shell with her, using it later to scoop up water from the river.

HOMINID FAMILY The social life of the earliest hominids was probably much like that of chimpanzees, with mutual grooming an important means of cementing personal relationships.

This one small invention is part of a long process of change for the hominids. Over the generations that follow, they learn to hunt animals such as hares and ground squirrels – wily, fast-moving prey that require a greater degree of cooperation and coordination from the hunters.

INVENTION AND IMAGINATION

By watching baboons digging in the ground, they discover that there are fat tubers and nourishing bulbs there. Their own hands, poorly equipped with short flat fingernails, prove less adept at digging than the sharply pointed nails of baboons, and their attempts to get at the tubers are only partially successful. In frustration, they try scratching at the soil with sharp pieces of stone, and with sticks. A broken acacia branch, with a hard sharp point where the wood has splintered away from the trunk, proves to be the most useful tool, and they consume some juicy tubers as a reward for their ingenuity. In the future, sharp-ended sticks such as this are sought out and treasured.

Hundreds of generations pass before the next innovation occurs. It happens in a particularly arid, treeless zone where there is a shortage of sticks for digging – none can be found with a suitable point. The hominids try digging with a blunt-ended stick, but it is useless. Later, as they rest in the shade of a rocky outcrop at midday, one hominid may try rubbing the blunt-ended stick against the rough corrugations of the rock. It wears away the wood, sharpening the stick into a pointed digging tool.

The next step takes many more generations: instead of a rocky outcrop, a sharp stone held in the hand is used to shape a digging stick. Sharp stones can be found in most areas, produced by the natural weathering of rock, but in a new area that the hominids colonise, many years later, they find only smooth, water-worn pebbles. It takes a leap of imagination for a hominid to think of smashing two of these pebbles together, in the hope of breaking one and producing a sharp edge.

The experiment works and the hominids are now makers of stone tools. In time, they learn to strike the stones together in a particular way that consistently produces a usable tool.

THE TOOLMAKERS

Later, they refine their techniques by chipping repeatedly at these simple tools to make the cutting edge both longer and sharper. This final innovation is just part of a long continuum of invention for the early hominids, but for the archaeologists of today it represents a major advance. An expert eye can distinguish tools that have been repeatedly chipped from stones that have been fragmented by natural processes – with the result that this moment is a milestone in the archaeological record. It was passed 2.5 million years ago, in Africa, the crucible of human evolution.

A million years have passed since this story first began – since one of those very early hominids, *Australopithecus afarensis*, experimented with using a piece of ostrich egg as a spoon. Humans have changed physically in these million years, but they are only a little different in appearance from *afarensis*, less ape-like facially, with somewhat larger brains. Their exact identity is a subject of heated debate, but they are generally referred to as *Homo habilis*, and assumed to be our direct ancestors.

Homo habilis shared the African landscape with three or more other species of hominid. These were smaller-brained and had probably not learned to make stone tools, although they may have used digging sticks. Some were very heavily built, with massive jaws and teeth; these massive hominids, known as 'robust australopithecines', depended largely on tubers for food. We know this from microscopic examination of their teeth, which reveals scratches made by gritty soil consumed with their food. In time these small-brained species died out, probably through competition with the more intelligent and inventive *Homo habilis*.

SCAVENGERS AND HUNTERS

Stone tools opened up a whole new world of possibilities. The hominids often encountered animal carcasses. Some of these kills had been made by lions or sabre-tooth tigers, and others were the result of drought. With sharp little flakes of stone, knocked from the side of a pebble, *Homo habilis* found that he could hack through the thick hide of these carcasses and cut away lumps of meat from within. One archaeological site in northern Kenya shows that a group of hominids found a dead hippopotamus and butchered it with stone tools.

Over the next million years, there were further increases in brain size among the descendants of *Homo habilis*. They also changed physically, becoming taller, with shorter arms in proportion to their legs and torso – a reflection of the fact that they no longer climbed trees so frequently. By about 1.5 million years ago, their bodies had changed so much that they resembled our own, although the head was far from modern, with a jutting face and massive bony ridges above the eyes. These hominids are known as *Homo ergaster* in Africa, but as *Homo erectus* in Asia and other parts of the world to which they migrated.

TOOLS AND HUTS

Hand-in-hand with the physical changes and growing brain size, there were improvements in the making of stone tools, culminating in a type of tool known as a handaxe – an almond-shaped implement that could hack, cut or scrape, as required. The handaxe was a major landmark because it was made to a standardised design, unlike the more pragmatic little tools of earlier generations – the rough fragments and shattered cobbles. With the handaxe there is a sense that the toolmaker has predetermined the shape that he imposes on the stone; and that this process has required far more discipline, skill and planning than ever before.

Most importantly, the handaxe design was shared by thousands of different toolmakers, not just in Africa but over large areas of Europe and Asia, too. At some sites, there are dozens of these tools, many unused. This sharing of tool design is the first hard evidence for a shared way of thinking and seeing which depends, not on instinct and inherited behaviour patterns, but on ideas that are handed down by teaching and example from one generation to the next.

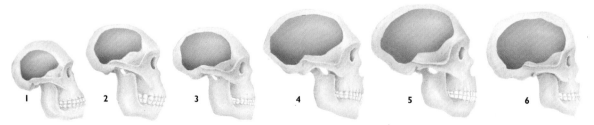

SKULL SHAPE AND BRAIN SIZE 1 *Australopithecus afarensis*. 2 *Homo habilis*. 3 *Homo erectus*. 4 *Homo sapiens*. 5 Neanderthal. 6 Modern. The modern brain is larger and more complex than that of the early hominids.

ALL-PURPOSE TOOL A collection of handaxes, the preferred tool of *Homo erectus*, made to a standard pattern.

There is little doubt that these humans had powers of speech, which were essential for teaching younger members of the group, although certain features of their chest and neck suggest that they were less precise and articulate in sound production than we are today.

These handaxe makers had also mastered the use of fire, which allowed them to penetrate cold areas as far distant as southern Britain and the area of China around Beijing. If there were no caves available, they may sometimes have built a shelter for themselves, using a framework of sturdy branches, with more slender leafy branches propped around it. This simple hut would be built within a ring of heavy stones to keep the branches in place. Remains of such a shelter have been found in the south of France, at a site called Terra Amata, which is now part of the modern town of Nice.

At Terra Amata, there are also traces of red ochre, a type of red-coloured clay that can be used to decorate the skin. The ochre was spread across the floor of the hut, so that the hominids and their shelter were both identified by the red colour, and a footprint has also been found leaving an ochre-tinted impression.

All this may point to an interest in matters beyond mere survival, to a self-consciousness that is capable of contemplating the human body and trying to modify its appearance, and perhaps to an abstract idea of 'home', in which the colour of the ochre symbolises the links between individuals and their base camp. Perhaps the red colour symbolised the fire in their hearth which, at night, marked out the shelter from the dark landscape.

Homo erectus survived for a remarkably long period of time – until about 200 000 years ago – without very much change in physical form or in the size of the brain.

THE FINAL STAGE

What happened next is difficult to say. A complex pattern of change is seen in Africa, Europe and Asia, with new and far more varied tools emerging, and relatively rapid changes in facial features, with steady increases in brain size. There was no simple line of change anywhere in the world, as far as the fossil record shows.

In western Europe, two distinctive types of people evolved, firstly *Homo sapiens neanderthalis* (Neanderthals) with heavy brow ridges but large brains, and secondly, but not long afterwards, people who looked more like ourselves, and who are sometimes

---

BRAINBOX

Despite the popular image of the Neanderthals as shambling and stupid, the Neanderthal brain was actually slightly larger than ours today. The extra capacity may be explained by the fact that their bodies were a little larger than ours – and bigger bodies need bigger brains.

---

referred to as Cro-Magnons. The direct antecedents of the Cro-Magnons seem either to have moved into Europe from elsewhere and eventually replaced the Neanderthals, or absorbed them into their own population – two scenarios which are still vigorously debated by anthropologists.

In Africa and Asia, a group of more modern people gradually appear in the fossil record, but whether they replaced the existing *Homo erectus* populations, or evolved from them, is unknown. Some new evidence from the DNA (genetic material) of living people has been interpreted as showing that modern people, *Homo sapiens*, evolved in Africa and then moved outwards to conquer the rest of the world. Not everyone agrees with this theory, however, and there is evidence to indicate that the gradual evolution of *erectus* into *sapiens* took place all over the inhabited world, with regular migrations providing a flow of genes between the different populations – with the result that the human race remained one species worldwide. There are certain continuities between the *erectus* populations of long ago and modern people in the same region – such as minor variations in the teeth of east Asian people, which they share with the ancient *erectus* hominids found near Beijing – that make this seem likely.

Whatever the precise truth, we do know that by 40 000 years ago, the world was populated only by people with large brain capacities – equivalent to those of today. In western Europe, there were the Neanderthals, on the one hand, and the Cro-Magnons or *Homo sapiens sapiens* on the other.

Elsewhere in the world at this time, there seems to have been only one dominant group, the truly modern people, *Homo sapiens sapiens*. These people habitually lived in caves or shelters of their own making; they used fire, hunted large animals, and wore fur clothing in colder areas. Their tools were exquisitely made from stone. Unlike their predecessors, they buried some of their dead, but not all of them. They continued to use red ochre, probably for painting their bodies. In some parts of the world, they had learned to make rafts or simple boats and were using these to explore new lands: already, they had sailed from South-east Asia to Australia. It is at this point, 40 000 years ago, that the story of this book begins.

CONQUERING THE ENVIRONMENT

The journey from ape to human took millions of years.

A crucial part of that journey involved gaining mastery over the physical

environment, turning darkness to light, and creating warmth and shelter in

inhospitable climates. The more our ancestors succeeded at such tasks, the farther

they could migrate from their tropical homelands. And the farther they went, the

greater the challenges, spurring them on to yet more ingenuity and resourcefulness.

ICE AND FIRE

At the height of the last ice age, some 18 000 years ago, vast sheets of ice

covered much of North America and Europe. At hardly any other time in human

history was the domestication of fire so essential.

THE AIR is so cold that, as the men exhale, their breath freezes and beads of ice collect on their beards. It is dark by the time they reach their home, a group of four huts built of mammoth skulls and bones, and covered with skins. The huts are sited beside a river on the Central Russian Plain, a bleak, windswept, treeless landscape. Pushing aside the skins that hang in the doorway of a hut, they smell the dense smoke and feel the warmth of the fire. It scorches the skin of their faces as they squat around it, the melting ice dripping from their wolf-skin clothes. Without fire, these people could not possibly survive in this extreme climate. The edge of the polar ice sheet is only a few hundred miles to the north, and is inching closer every year.

The whole world was profoundly influenced by the ice ages, repeated cycles of cooling and warming that began about 1.5 million years ago and ceased (perhaps only temporarily) 10 000 years ago. During times of glaciation, the Arctic ice sheets advanced across Europe, Asia and North America; glaciers descended from mountain tops into the valleys; sea levels fell because so much water was locked up in the ice sheets; and forests in the Northern Hemisphere retreated, to be replaced by the sparse grasslands known as steppe. Farther north, the steppe itself was replaced by tundra – ground-hugging vegetation made up of lichens and shrubby cold-resistant plants such as dwarf willows.

During the warm periods between ice ages – the interglacials – the climate was usually a little colder than it is today. The sea levels gradually rose, inundating areas that had once been coastal fishing sites or camping grounds, so that, from generation to generation, people had to adapt to a steadily changing landscape. Fossilised bones found beneath modern London show that, 100 000 years ago, at the

MAMMOTH BUILDINGS
With no wood, the people of the Central Russian Plain had to build their huts with the bones and hides of mammoths.

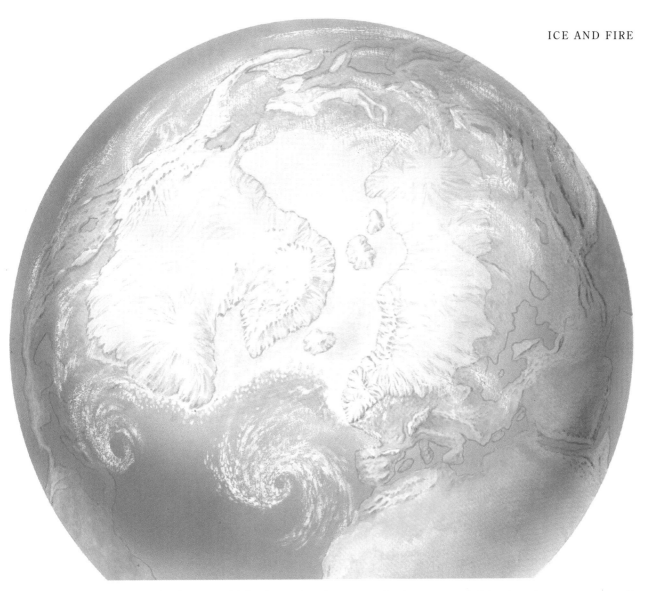

MARCH OF THE ICE **The polar ice cap, which advanced and retreated, is shown at the height of the ice ages.**

height of one interglacial, the area had a subtropical climate with hippopotamuses wallowing in the River Thames.

Although the ice ages affected human life everywhere in the world, no inhabited zone could rival the Central Russian Plain for sheer numbing intensity of cold between about 25 000 and 10 000 years ago. Frostbite would have been a constant danger, and one that could kill the healthiest person in a matter of hours: if chilled fingers or toes become deprived of blood for long enough, then the tissue dies and turns black.

As the hunters thaw out, gently rubbing their fingertips to restore the blood flow, a child comes in with more bones for the fire. This is their fuel: the huge bones of mammoths stripped of their flesh and stored in underground pits until needed. The bones are difficult to set alight, so a fire is kept burning night and day, carefully tended to prevent it going out.

When they first arrived at this winter encampment, travelling here from their summer home, they had to kindle a new fire in the hearth. Perhaps they laid a bed of dry leaves and woody stems, carefully collected and brought with them. On top of this they probably spread a layer of dry brittle fungus. To make a spark, one of them may have struck a piece of flint against a nodule of a mineral known as iron pyrites.

FEEDING THE FIRE

The flint and ironstone clashed together again and again, until eventually a spark fell on the kindling and it began to burn. A lump of white fat, cut from a large carcass, may have been added to make the flames burn more brightly. The woody stems caught light, and the first small bones were laid on top. Larger bones were then added, until the fire was thoroughly aflame.

There is no doubt that fire was central to the lives of these people. Fire kept them warm, and warded off frostbite and dangerous animals such as bears. It allowed them to cook their food, to preserve skins and furs, and to smoke fish caught in the river. In the summer, when mosquitoes and midges formed black swarms in the air, smoke from the camp fires would have kept them at bay. But it would also have had a bad effect on the lungs of these people, living in unventilated huts. A hacking cough was probably so common 22 000 years ago that people simply took it for granted as part of the human condition.

The Ice Age Diet

The ice ages profoundly affected the diet of these people, for there was little to eat in the tundra except meat and fish. Some of the low-growing plants produced small berries and, as summer drew to a close, there may have been mushrooms in the small patches of forest that survived in the warmer valleys. But for the most part, flesh and fat were the sole foods. Small burrowing animals known as marmots were the main source of meat, but larger animals such as horses and reindeer (caribou) were also hunted. No one knows if mammoths were hunted and eaten, or if the bones used in building the huts came from mammoths that had died of natural causes.

Tundra landscapes rest upon permafrost – a layer of permanently frozen, rock-hard soil which lies a short distance below the surface. It acts as a barrier in the earth, through which rainwater and snowmelt cannot pass, so that there are innumerable ponds and boggy patches on the surface in summer.

These were rich breeding grounds for mosquitoes and other biting flies, but as compensation, some water birds such as gulls, crakes, rails and plovers came here to nest; their eggs may well have been collected and eaten, providing a welcome change in the diet. The habit of storing food, which developed during the ice ages, may have changed human society. Once people became dependent on the stores, and life revolved around them, then they were tied, both to the stores and to the group which had made them. People had to stay together come what may. We can guess that this situation would have led to a more rigid code of conduct, a greater criticism of other people's behaviour, and less room for individuality. Rules and customs would have been one way of minimising disputes between people and controlling the eruption of tempers in difficult circumstances.

A Secure Base

The elaborate huts made of mammoth bones and skulls may be evidence of such social changes – for it would have taken energy and organisation to build these shelters. One archaeologist has estimated that building an encampment with four large dwellings would occupy ten full-time workers for 17 days. They would have to shift more than 130 000 lb (60 000 kg) of mammoth bones in the process. These encampments must have been the work of people who knew they would stay together.

The huts, so solid and permanent, also tied people to the land itself. The archaeological evidence shows that some of these huts were re-occupied at regular intervals, perhaps by the same group returning each winter. The dwellings stood firmly in the landscape, the handiwork of humankind. The

Monarch of the Ice Age Like many other giant mammals of the ice ages, the mammoth became extinct when the world grew warmer once again.

MANY WAYS TO MAKE A FIRE

THE EARLIEST FIRE-MAKERS struck stones together to produce a spark but, in time, other methods were developed. One of the most valuable was to create fire with friction. In theory this can be done by rubbing two sticks together, but a more efficient method is to use a fire drill. At its simplest, this consists of a flat piece of wood with a circular hollow and a wooden rod which fits into that hollow. The rod is rubbed vigorously between the palms of the hands, so that it rotates rapidly in the hollow.

Fire-making with a fire drill can require two people, one to hold the base plate, and the other to turn the stick. A one-person version is also known, where the stick is rotated by moving a bow backwards and forwards, the string of the bow coiled around the stick to make it rotate.

The rubbing of the rod against the base plate generates heat by friction, and the heat eventually becomes intense enough to set fire to the end of the rod. The rod can then be used to light kindling material, such as very dry leaves or tinder fungus.

Some fire drills have been found in prehistoric sites, but whether we would recognise a fire drill if we found one is a debatable question. Anthropologists have described a multipurpose tool made by certain Australian Aborigines in the recent past. This wooden platter has a small circular depression and was employed in four different ways. Although used as the base plate of a fire drill, it also acted as a dish for food, as a digging tool for obtaining plant roots, and as a spear-thrower: the butt of the

FIRE DRILLING A fire drill relies on the heat produced by friction to start a blaze, but successful use of the implement requires considerable skill.

spear was fitted onto the peg of wood or bone at one end of the platter, causing the spear to rotate when thrown and thereby giving the weapon greater accuracy. For

the nomadic Aborigine, having one tool which served four different purposes, and therefore reduced the load to be carried, was a considerable practical advantage.

people who inhabited them may have been among the first to feel a strong sense of identity with their local environment – a landscape of which they were permanent elements, not nomadic wanderers drifting randomly through with the breeze.

TEMPERED BY THE FLAMES

Fire, like ice, shaped human behaviour. Learning to handle it safely was a crucial aspect of the domestication of fire – a process that occurred more than 300 000 years ago and perhaps as much as 1.5 million years ago.

As long as people lived in small huts or tents and lit their camp fires outside, the dangers of fire were

HOLDING FIRE

Some human groups discovered by anthropologists in the 19th century did not know how to make a fire. They relied upon fire created by lightning strikes or volcanic eruptions which they kept alive in a hearth, or as glowing embers that were carried from place to place. The very earliest hominids to use fire probably could not make it for themselves, but preserved it in the same way.

easily contained. But once they began to build solid and substantial houses, fire became dangerous once more. The construction of a hearth, a ring of stones within which the fire was laid, may well have been an attempt to control the fire by limiting its size, thus minimising the dangers. Caution and

self-discipline were required of children even from an early age, and this too must have changed the nature of human life, if not human nature itself.

One way of controlling the height of the flames was to have several small fires instead of one large one. This was obviously the practice in a hut excavated at Pincevent in France. Three hearths were found in a row, allowing the inhabitants a fireside seat, but keeping each fire small and controllable.

The risks of fire tended to increase as time went by and housing became more elaborate. In Iron Age Denmark, individual houses, or sometimes whole villages, regularly burned to the ground. These houses were framed of timber, with the walls built up from peat turf, and the roof thatched with straw or dry heather.

This combustible mixture could turn into an inferno in minutes. A red-hot spark rising in the smoke could quickly set light to the roof, and because the houses in a village were built so close together, the fire could leap from roof to roof. The excavated remains of burned-out dwellings, still complete with their kitchen utensils and charred items of

BEATING ICE WITH FIRE Over 5000 years ago, a lone traveller died on this mountain pass in the Alps. His belongings included the means of starting a camp fire – essential in this icy environment.

food, are a testament to such devastating fires. In some Iron Age dwellings, there are signs of new methods to control fire. Certain houses from this region have the remains of clay structures built into the floor, which are thought to be ovens. Experimental reconstructions show that they contained the fire and made it safer, while still providing ample heat. They worked best with green wood and may have served to smoke food as well as warm the house.

Fire was the means by which Iron Age people extracted iron from its ores. It was also essential in making pottery. The dry clay, moulded into a pot, but still brittle and useless before firing, became a sturdy and waterproof material.

The use of fire in shaping and changing materials was by no means new. From the earliest times, people had known that it could be used to shape wood far more quickly than a stone tool could do. One method was to burn a piece of wood in the fire, allow it to cool, then scrape away the blackened area. The process would be repeated over and over again until the desired shape was achieved. Stone, too, could be modified by the heat of a fire. Very hard or unwieldy stones that needed to be broken could be placed in a fire and heated, then cooled suddenly with water. The heating and rapid cooling produced a sudden cracking in the rock, shattering it into usable parts.

It is difficult to know whether fire was used for cooking from the very first. Sure signs of cooking in the fossil record include the leg bones of animals, broken open for their marrow. An uncooked bone can only be split open lengthwise and it is a difficult job, but a cooked bone can be snapped in half far more easily and the marrow sucked out.

COOKING FOOD

Long before cereals were grown by the first farmers, seeds of wild grasses were roasted and eaten. About 12 000 years ago, in the area known as the 'Fertile Crescent' which encompasses modern Turkey, Iran and Iraq, hunter-gatherers were using the seeds of grasses as a source of food. They had already learned to grind the grass seeds on special stones to make flour, which may then have been made into thin unleavened bread and baked. Once agriculture became established in this area, bread became a central part of the diet. Baking bread has always been a skilled business, and the careful control of temperature on the hearthstone or in the bread oven would have been of crucial importance.

Much the same happened in the Far East where

HUNTING WITH FIRE **The natural fear which animals have of fire makes it an invaluable tool for human hunters.**

A NEOLITHIC HUNTER IN THE ITALIAN ALPS

ABOUT 5300 YEARS AGO, a lone hunter set out from his village in what is now northern Italy, and headed up into the Alps. He was injured and in pain from several broken ribs, and he travelled poorly equipped for the mountains, with just a bow, some arrows, a copper-headed axe and a few simple stone tools. Although he had little in the way of food, he did take with him the means of starting a camp fire. Packed into a cylindrical container, made of birch bark, were glowing embers of wood. The embers had been wrapped in damp grass and sycamore leaves to prevent them from setting light to the container.

Studies of modern nomadic people show that this is a simple way of starting a camp fire. Insulated by the leaves, and deprived of oxygen in the container, the ember stays hot for many hours. Blowing on the dull red glow of the ember quickly stirs it into flame again, so that it can be used to light a new fire at the next stopping place. As a back-up, the hunter also carried the means to start a fire from scratch. This fire-making

FROZEN IN TIME Emerging from a glacier, the 'man in the ice' still had his clothing and equipment intact.

kit consisted of pieces of the true tinder fungus, *Fomes fomentarius*, cut from a birch or beech tree, and some iron pyrites for creating a spark. Finds from Neolithic graves reveal the other items that may have been in the birch container but have been lost. These would have included a small flint knife for cutting the tinder fungus from a tree, a piece of flint for striking the

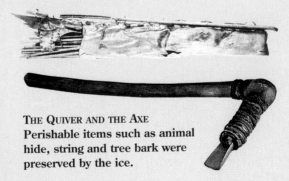

THE QUIVER AND THE AXE Perishable items such as animal hide, string and tree bark were preserved by the ice.

iron pyrites to produce a spark, a shell in which the tinder fungus would be loosened into a fluffy mass, and an implement made of bone for loosening the fungus. In evidence from grave finds, only men carried such kit.

In the event, the hunter never reached a place where he could strike camp and make a fire. He may have been overtaken by a blizzard, or dense fog, and forced to shelter under a rock ledge. Here he ate some dried ibex meat, and tried to stay awake, for to fall asleep was certain death. He was too exhausted to succeed. He lay down on his left side, trying to get comfortable despite his broken ribs. He drifted into sleep and soon his clothes froze to the ground. The man died without ever waking, and a huge fall of snow buried him before the morning came. He had clung on to the birch container with its embers until the very last moment, but before he died they had fallen from his hand.

The body, covered by its blanket of snow, was mummified and preserved in this way, to become encased in the ice of a glacier, emerging some 5300 years later, in September 1991.

rice was domesticated and became the staple crop, and in the Americas where maize assumed a similar role. Although neither of these cereals requires such complex preparation as wheat, fire was the essential mediator in making them edible.

Each of these innovations, while it improved human life, also brought a new form of dependency. It became increasingly difficult for an individual to survive alone, or for a small group to split off and go its own way, because the skills required to

A Bronze Age Cookhouse

Roasting meat was a simple business in prehistoric times. It could be suspended over a fire on a wooden spit, or placed directly in the glowing embers. Another method, probably used by Neanderthal people, was to set stone slabs in a fire, allow the slabs to become red hot, then brush away the embers and place the meat, cut into slices, onto the red-hot stone.

The meat of older animals is tough, and requires boiling to make it chewable. This was a far more difficult procedure at a time when cooking pots made of metals or pottery were not available. In Bronze Age Ireland, at a place known as Ballyvourney in County Cork, a simple solution to the problem was found. The ground here is waterlogged and people dug a trough to a depth of 16 in (40 cm), making it just over a yard (1 m) wide and 6 ft (1.8 m) long. This large trough was lined with wood, and automatically filled up with water from the surrounding peaty soil. Several hearths were built close to the trough, and nearby was a hut in which stood a rack for holding meat and a rough wooden table for butchering the carcasses.

In an attempt to discover how this arrangement might have worked, archaeologists set out to cook a leg of mutton weighing 11 lb (5 kg), using only materials available at the time. They wrapped the mutton in straw to keep it clean, and built fires in each of the hearths. Once the fires were roaring brightly, stones were placed to heat up in the embers. When these were red hot, they were pushed out of the hearth, using damp sticks which would not catch fire, and knocked into the wooden trough. A number of red-hot stones were added, and after half an hour the water in the trough began to boil. At this point, the leg of mutton was added.

More hot stones were added at intervals, sufficient to keep the water boiling. After three and a half hours, the leg of mutton was taken out and found to be cooked through, with an excellent flavour.

maintain life had become so specialised and varied, and because the material infrastructure – kilns and bread ovens, crucibles and smithies – could not easily be reconstructed elsewhere.

CONQUERING THE DARKNESS

In time, fire was used specifically for producing light by means of burning torches and lamps. Evidence of torch use has been found at Salts Cave, Kentucky, USA, where bundles of reed canes have been found, held together by twines of strong grass or strips of bark. The same plants that were used then still grow in the area today, and archaeologists have used them to reconstruct the ancient torches. Taking them into a cave to light their way, they noted that the smoke made black smudges on the low roof of the cave, which looked exactly like marks dating from the time of the original occupants, many thousands of years ago. However, they also found that their eyes and noses watered badly within the confines of the cave. This discomfort was increased by the hot embers that fell from

POTBOILERS The use of red-hot stones to bring water to the boil and keep it simmering survived until quite recent times, and is the origin of the expression 'potboilers'.

the torches to the ground. They concluded that prehistoric people were a great deal hardier than we are today and far more tolerant of intense physical discomfort.

In some of the decorated caves of France, which were painted as many as 30 000 years ago, dozens of lamps have been found. These are fairly crude, consisting of nothing more than a flat or slightly hollow stone. Animal fat, collected from a roasting carcass, was placed in the hollow, and twigs added to act as a wick. In a few of the French caves, the lamps are more elaborate – carved out of soft stone, such as sandstone, with a broad hollow part where the tallow was lit, and a longer narrower

handle with decorative carved marks. At Grime's Graves flint mine in Britain, which dates from 4500 years ago, rough hemispherical lumps of chalk, hollowed out to hold burning fat, were used to illuminate the miners' work.

In attempts to re-create Stone Age lamps, archaeologists discovered that the best results were obtained by setting moss alight to melt the fat in the lamp. The most efficient wicks were those that had been specially prepared from juniper twigs, by drying the twigs and then soaking them in the fat from roasted meat. In later eras, when the manufacture of string from twisted plant fibres was commonplace, this was undoubtedly used as a wick.

In the Fertile Crescent of the Near East, the stories of ice and fire intertwine once more. As the ice ages came to an end about 10 000 years ago, the people of the Fertile Crescent were confronted with some relatively rapid and potentially threatening changes in their homelands.

SHAPING THE LANDSCAPE WITH FIRE

Glaciers and ice sheets were melting far away in distant lands, but sea levels rose all over the world, drowning areas that had once provided people with a good livelihood. The people were forced into a smaller area, but at the same time, as temperatures rose, the grassy plains of the Fertile Crescent began to be invaded by bushes and pioneering young trees. And so they used fire to knock back the scrub and saplings, and to encourage young grass to grow. From manipulating the vegetation with

THE ART OF FIRE

Two of the most important materials used in prehistoric art were made by fire. Red ochre is formed by baking a yellow clay that contains mineral salts. The heat transforms the yellow minerals into red. Charcoal is made by burning wood without sufficient air present, so that it does not turn to ash, but retains its original structure. Fragments of charcoal can be found among the ashes of most camp fires. Charcoal was used as a black pigment in cave paintings.

fire, it was only a short step to planting the grasses and thus becoming the first farmers.

As agriculture spread around the world, fire continued to be used as a tool for land management, for clearing new land, killing off weeds in established fields, and exterminating pests and diseases before they could infest new crops.

The use of fire also produced changes in the landscape by a more indirect means. In most areas, wood was the obvious fuel, and the demand for wood placed a heavy burden on the forests. Deforestation undoubtedly occurred in some areas in prehistoric times, which led in turn to more grassland and scrub. Changes in the animal population followed, sometimes creating new sources of food, at other times eliminating an important tree-loving species upon which people relied, such as the common honeybee.

NATURE'S FIRE In dry terrain, some fires begin naturally, ignited as a flash of lightning strikes tinder-dry grass or trees. The first use of fire by hominids relied on such natural sources.

ARTIFICIAL LIGHT **The earliest lamps used animal fat, or tallow, to provide a flickering light.**

In areas where wood was scarce or non-existent, alternative fuels, such as antler and bone, had to be found. Animal dung can also be burned as long as it is dried well in advance, and this cheap fuel, which is still widely used in parts of the world such as India, may have been exploited by prehistoric fire-makers.

There is clear evidence of a shortage of wood by the time of the Iron Age in northern Europe. In areas such as Jutland, where there are extensive peat bogs, the use of peat for fuel had begun by this time. Special wooden spades were used to dig the peat. It must then have been stacked, as it is today in Ireland, and allowed to dry before being added to the fire. The clouds of brown smoke given off by the peat fires may have spurred people to make smoke holes in their roofs, thereby reducing the air pollution that they had to endure.

Smoke may be obnoxious, but it can have its uses. Some of the earliest written records, from the ancient civilisation of Mesopotamia over 4000 years ago, mention the use of fire in fumigating houses to kill off fleas, lice, bed bugs, cockroaches and other vermin. 'Smoking out' may also have been used to evict rabbits and foxes from their burrows.

On a more sinister note, smoke could have been used as a weapon against other human groups. People sheltering deep within caves may have been smoked out by rival tribes. Fire itself was also an instrument of terror, and attackers wielding flaming torches were probably part of human rivalry and warfare many thousands of years ago.

By the time of the Iron Age in Britain, 2600 years ago, when much of the population was living in massively defended hill-forts to escape any potential aggressors, fire became a major force of destruction. Many of the hill-forts were attacked by archers who may have launched thousands of burning arrows over the defensive ramparts, setting light to the wooden houses within.

At Hembury hill-fort in Devon, the massive oak timbers of the gateways and houses were all burned. Some fell into the ditch that surrounded the hill-fort and continued to blaze furiously there. The fire was so hot that it discoloured the rock beneath, and the flames must have leapt high into the night sky. Archaeologists found a layer of charcoal in the ditch which was a minimum of 6 in (15 cm) thick all the way around the fort, and up to 2 ft (60 cm) thick in places. Throughout their lives, fire had kept these people warm, cooked their food, and created their iron axes, but in the end it had destroyed them.

SMOKED FOOD, AN ANCIENT DELICACY

To SMOKE FOOD, green wood was placed on a fire – a sure way of generating ample smoke. This was almost certainly done outside, or in a special oven, because the smoke would have been unbearable to breathe. Smoking food was a slow business and even before it began, food had to be dried in the sun to ensure that it did not rot. Careful planning and preparation were required, but the reward was food that could last for months and was good to eat, especially if the right wood was chosen. Today we eat smoked food for its wonderful taste – a link with our predecessors of 20 000 years ago.

Immortal Hunter A cave painting from the Sahara preserves the image of a hunter who lived 9000 years ago.

MAKING CLOTHING

The first needles, made of bone some 20 000 years ago, were a significant step

towards a warmer life; and it was not long before decorated clothes, elaborate hairstyles and

simple jewellery began to serve an ornamental – as well as a practical – function.

THE WOMAN selects a reindeer leg bone from the pile set aside for making tools – bones that have been cleaned and dried in the sun. Carefully, she scratches two long straight lines close together on the bone, using a sharp flint tool. With the point of the flint, she makes the scratches deeper and deeper until they become two parallel grooves.

She works slowly and thoughtfully because she is trying out a completely new idea. She scratches some more, and then joins up the two lines, bringing them together in a sharp point at one end and joining them with a rounded arc at the other end. Near the rounded end, she bores into the bone with the point of the flint, making a small circular depression. Finally, she cuts into the grooves at an angle, so that they meet and the splinter of bone is set free. She holds it up to the light, between her two fingers, to check that the circular hole goes right through the bone. It does. She is holding the very first needle.

She walks back to the corner of the rock shelter where her sister sits making clothes, laboriously puncturing holes in the reindeer skin, and pushing thongs made of animal sinew through the holes, using a sliver of bone. It is these slivers, employed for generations to push thread through holes in this way, that have inspired the woman's new invention. By adding a hole at one end of the bone splinter, as she now demonstrates to her sister, they can thread the sinew into the needle and pull it through the hole instead of pushing – a far more efficient and speedy process.

INDIRECT EVIDENCE FOR CLOTHES

The first needle-maker probably lived about 20 000 years ago in western Europe, then still in the grip of the ice ages. The reason that needles are such an important source of evidence is that clothes themselves are perishable, except in certain very rare conditions. We have absolutely no evidence of the first use of unsewn furs to cover the human body, and no indication of when or where this occurred, because furs rot quickly and are lost.

Cloth also decomposes rapidly, except in arid environments such as deserts, or in very dry caves, or when immersed in a peat bog where the water is acid and lacks oxygen, with the result that bacteria cannot destroy it. Peat water is also rich in natural tannins

USING A FLINT KNIFE
To provide as big a hide as possible, it is removed in a strict sequence of cuts, with the feet removed first. The hide is then hung to dry, usually over a smoky fire which helps preservation.

which colour the water a rich brown and assist preservation. In a peat bog, woollen fabric, leather and hide clothing all survive remarkably well, although linen rots away.

For most of prehistory, however, there is no sign of the clothes themselves, and hard evidence such as that of needles, spindles and weaving implements has to serve instead. Brooches and pins, used for holding cloaks and shawls, are also informative.

DID PREHISTORIC PEOPLE WEAR SHOES?

Occasionally there is other indirect evidence. In the decorated caves of south-west France, footprints are sometimes found, made in what was once wet clay. All the prints are of bare feet, with no evidence of any footwear. It seems almost inconceivable that, when the ground was often thick with frost, Ice Age people would not have thought to make shoes for themselves, despite their considerable skill at making hide clothing. Is it possible that they wore shoes outside, but took them off inside the caves? This seems unlikely since caves were damp and cold, and the burning torches used to light the way dropped hot embers onto the cave floor. It is possible then that if Ice Age Europeans went barefoot in the caves they also went barefoot outside, ignoring discomfort

PIERCING INSIGHT The needle, like the wheel, was an invention so perfect in its simplicity that it has survived in virtually the same form to the present day. The bone needles of prehistory, $1^1/_2$-$4^1/_2$ in (4-12 cm) long were sharpened on pieces of flint.

that we would find intolerable. Perhaps they valued the firm grip on rocks and hillsides which bare feet gave them.

Indirect evidence of another kind comes from Sungir, on the Russian Plain near present-day Moscow. Some 23 000 years ago, a man of about 60 was buried along with two boys, one aged about eight and the other about 11. When the bodies were excavated, curious snaking lines extended from side to side across the skeletons – lines made up of thousands of tiny beads. At first the archaeologists were puzzled, until it occurred to them that the beads must have been sewn onto the clothing.

So heavily decorated was each garment that the beads revealed a great deal about its shape. There were caps decorated with beads and, in the case of the old man, with the canine teeth of foxes. All three wore trousers and tunics and, on their feet, shoes – those luxuries that

FUR AND GRASS The seams of this fur garment were mended with threads of twisted grass. The fur has long since fallen out, and it now resembles leather.

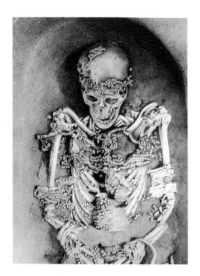

BEARDED CHIEFTAIN The old man of Sungir was reduced to nothing but beads and bones by 35 000 years of decay; the beads were made of ivory, shell and fox teeth.

the people of western Europe may not have possessed. It was certainly very cold on the Central Russian Plain, and the risk of frostbite to the toes was high.

This burial was excavated with care and, by looking closely, archaeologists were able to see the marks made in the underlying soil by folds in the garments: the soil had hardened over the millennia, preserving these folds for ever. There is little doubt that the clothes were made from animal skins, presumably skins with short hair, such as those of wolves or hares, since beadwork would have been lost to view among luxuriant furs.

What is particularly interesting about the Sungir burials is that the beads themselves represented a colossal investment of time and energy. Most were made from mammoth tusks, although a few were of shell. Modern attempts to make such beads, using only stone tools, have shown that each required about 15 minutes of intensive labour by someone well practised in the art. Yet the three bodies had over 10 000 beads in all – the total time required simply to

---

PREHISTORIC KNITTING

Knitting with two needles was unknown in prehistoric times, and may not have been invented until the 15th century. However, there was a technique known as *naalbinding* which used a single threaded needle. It seems to have been practised in Denmark over 6000 years ago, and was used for items such as socks.

---

make these beads was 2500 hours. If one person spent five hours of every day making beads, it would have taken them almost half a year to prepare all the beads for just one costume. Clearly everyone cannot have spent such huge amounts of time on bead-making, so they did not all dress so ornately.

The three beaded bodies must have been special people, whose clothes were made for them by other members of the group. Analysis of the style of the beads suggests that there were just three or four bead-makers, each with his or her particular technique.

If these expert craftworkers spent so much time making beads, then some of their food, tools and fuel must have been supplied by others in the group. All this has led some archaeologists to speculate that the old man was the leader of the group and a powerful, revered figure. Furthermore, they argue that the presence of the young boys in similarly rich attire implies that the position of chief was passed down from father to son. It is, they say, perhaps the first evidence we have for hierarchies in the history of humanity, and it fits in with the trend towards

---

MAKING CLOTH FROM BARK

PREHISTORIC PEOPLE on the islands of Polynesia, lacking any other suitable material for making cloth, invented a product using fibres of tree bark. Various trees could be used, but paper mulberry proved to be the most valuable. To make the cloth, a tree was felled and the bark stripped off. Pieces of bark were then soaked in vats of water and allowed to ferment – a process similar to that used for extracting linen thread from the flax plant.

After fermentation, the bark was beaten with wooden hammers on a smooth log until it produced a thin papery layer of white material.

Further treatment was required to make it more flexible and comfortable to wear, and the bark cloth was then decorated by painting with pigments. If necessary, pieces of bark cloth could be joined together by wetting and beating, to create larger strips of cloth: great pride was taken in producing huge sheets of cloth for ceremonial purposes.

PRECIOUS RESIN Amber is the fossilised resin of pine trees. Found in many parts of the world, it was valued for its beauty by prehistoric people. These necklaces come from Scandinavia.

group living suggested by the existence of food stores and sturdy dwellings on the Central Russian Plain at this time.

Another interesting aspect of the finds at Sungir is that clothing, even in the earliest times, had become something far more than a means of keeping warm. As well as serving practical ends, clothing was clearly expected to be ornamental, to act as a mark of status, or to identify individuals as members of the same group. Indeed, some clothing may have had no practical use at all. A small ivory figurine from France, known as 'The Lady of Brassempouy', had the face of a young girl, and long straight hair which seems to be covered by a delicate hairnet. Woven fabric was unknown in Europe at this time, about 25 000 years ago. The net was probably made by knotting together lengths of fine cord, manufactured from twisted plant fibres.

PREHISTORIC CARTOONS

Purely decorative headgear is also seen in engravings made on limestone blocks in the cave of La Marche, in the French Pyrenees. These engravings are more recent than the ivory Lady of Brassempouy, dating from about 16 000 years ago. The people who made the engravings were probably drawing portraits of each other – something that is very rare at other European sites of this age. The cartoon-like drawings show distinctive faces, full of character, often with deliberate styling of the hair. In most of the men depicted, it is cut short in a 'pudding-basin' style. Some of the heads are shown wearing hats which appear to be fashion garments rather than practical items. There is a headband on one of the figures, and several of those with long hair have it plaited, or coiled up into a bun. Belts and bracelets are also in evidence, emphasising the importance which these people laid upon personal ornamentation. Hair drawn up into a bun is also seen on a small ivory carving of a woman's head, from Dolni Vestonice in Moravia, which is probably 26 000 years old.

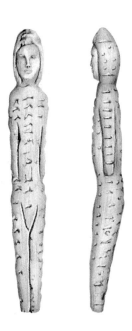

ERMINE ROBES The Buret figurine shows a man clad from head to toe in ermine; there are no apparent openings in the garment.

By contrast, the clothing shown on a figurine from Buret in Siberia is entirely practical. The carving dates from the Stone Age, and shows a man with beard and moustache dressed from top to toe in animal skins. The most interesting detail of the figure is the hood which covers the man's head and is joined to the other garments. This is the only firm prehistoric evidence of people wearing hoods, although common sense suggests that hoods would have been a very useful form of clothing and a natural development from holding animal skins over head and shoulders.

Chevron-shaped marks on the clothing may represent stitching or decoration. Alternatively, the clothing depicted here could have been made from ermine, the winter coat of a stoat, which is white except for the black tail tip. When ermine are skinned and the pelts sewn together, the overall effect is one of white fur with black chevron marks.

A puzzling feature of the Buret figurine is that no lines are engraved to indicate the bottom of the tunic or the top of the trousers. The clothing is shown as a one-piece suit. Is this simply the result of artistic licence, in which unimportant details are omitted?

Given the careful rendering of the beard, moustache and facial features, this seems unlikely. Perhaps the clothing shown on this figurine was actually a one-piece suit with a slit down front or back which was sewn up once the garment was on. As a certain means of keeping out icy winds, sewing up a garment has some advantages. In the 19th century, poor children in country areas of England were sewn into their winter vests for several months at a time. A thick layer of goose grease was applied to their skin first, as added protection from the cold.

If the Siberian hunter shown in the Buret figurine was really sewn into his clothes, how did he relieve himself? One clue may come from traditional Chinese clothing used for small children. Thick padded trousers were worn to keep out the winter cold, but there was a slit along the seam between the buttocks, so that bladder or

VANITY FAIR The young girl shown in the ivory figure from Brassempouy wore a delicate veil over her hair.

bowels could be emptied without removing any clothing. In the case of the Buret figurine, as in most artistic depictions, we can never be really sure what prehistoric people wore, but in trying to interpret the scant evidence, we should be wary of thinking only in terms of our familiar types of clothing.

The figurine from Buret and the sketchy engravings from La Marche are both rare finds in that they show clothed human beings. The major obsession of Stone Age artists in Europe was animals. They covered cave walls with paintings of horses and bison. They carved stones in the form of seals, fish and ibex. Occasionally they might show a mysterious half-human figure, with an animal's head or some other strange feature. And they carved statuettes of women with massive breasts, stomachs and thighs, who are usually naked or wearing a simple girdle.

continued on page 38

CLOTHES FROM THE PEAT BOGS

The most complete set of clothing worn by Ice Age people

has been preserved in the peat bogs of Denmark.

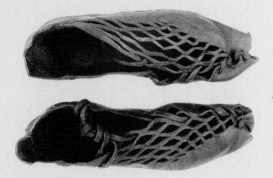

FINE FOOTWEAR
These leather shoes
display remarkable
craftsmanship and
sense of design.

STYLISH KNOTS Hairstyles were
often very elaborate in northern
Europe during the Iron Age.

ACID WATER and the lack of oxygen in a peat bog create ideal conditions for preserving clothing, as well as hair, skin and other soft parts of the body. Many Iron Age people have been discovered in the peat bogs of Denmark, including one at Huldre Fen, where a woman was found with a complete set of clothing. Next to her skin was a cape made of the softest lambskin, and she wore another of these as an outer garment. Her skirt, which was clasped to her body with a leather strap, was made of woollen cloth and had a plaid pattern. On her head was a scarf of the same plaid material, secured with a pin made of bird bone. She also had the Iron Age equivalent of a handbag, made from the bladder of an animal, which contained a woollen hairband and a leather strap. There was even a pocket in her skirt, containing a fine hair-comb made of animal horn.

Other finds from the Danish peat bogs have included leather shoes and sandals, open-work bonnets worn by women and secured with ribbons under the chin, skin capes covering the shoulders, which were worn mainly by men, and bronze pins, beads and other simple jewellery. The women's clothing often consists of huge quantities of woven woollen fabric, made into billowing skirts, or loose dresses. Some of the men are naked except for a skin cape, a leather cap and belt. It may be that they were wearing linen trousers and tunics as well, but that these have rotted in the peat water – linen is one of few fabrics to do so.

HEAVY SKIRTS Fabric was rarely
tailored, as this woollen skirt,
gathered around the waist, shows.

WELL GROOMED In her pocket,
the woman of Huldre Fen carried
a comb carved from animal horn.

WATERY GRAVE Iron Age communities used pools in the bogs for executions, and perhaps for human sacrifices.

Most curious of all are the hairstyles seen on several of the men. Their long hair was combed upwards, then coiled into an intricate and curious knot on one side of the head. Other men wore their hair in a small single plait, beginning at the top of the head and coiling about the back of the scalp. By contrast, women's hairstyles would look unremarkable today, the hair often being gathered up into a simple coil on the back of the head. One of the more complicated female hairstyles was found in a bog at Arden Forest in North Jutland. The body was that of a young woman, aged 20 to 25, who was laid in the bog wearing only a pretty net bonnet, although a piece of woven cloth lay over her, and another beneath her. The hair under the bonnet was a rich dark blonde in colour. It had been braided into two plaits which were tied with fine string at the ends. The plaits were then coiled up together on the back of her head.

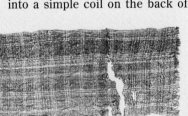

RICHLY ATTIRED Huldre Fen has provided a complete set of Iron Age clothes. The woman was wealthy and of high status. Her plaid scarf is shown above.

GIRL'S BONNET
This bonnet covered the blonde hair of the girl of Arden Forest.

Whether these represented goddesses or were simply idealised depictions of the human form, they tell us little about everyday clothing.

African cave artists were also obsessed by animal forms, painting giraffes, wild sheep, antelopes and ostriches, but they included human figures in their paintings as well. Sometimes these were so highly stylised as to give us little information about clothing, but in other cases the figures are semirealistic, and their garments clearly drawn.

One running figure wears what seems to be a short grass skirt, with bands of cloth about her ankles and wrists, and further broad bands on each of her upper arms. From these armbands, long trailing strands of grass or fine cord hang down past her waist. Trailing filaments also extend from the wristbands. Her body seems to be painted or tattooed in broad sweeping stripes, and on her head is a helmet with wide horns – or perhaps it is her hair, stiffened with clay or grease, and then sculpted into horn-like shapes, a technique that is still practised by some present-day African tribes. Clearly this dress is meant to impress, or to signify some ancient ritual, rather than to keep the wearer warm.

This painting was discovered at Tassili N'Ajjer, which is now in the Sahara Desert but was far less arid from at least 8000 years ago, when the paintings were begun. Surrounding Tassili N'Ajjer was a grassy plain, where large herds of animals roamed and fish swam in the rivers. The people swam in the river too, as the pictures show. They wore girdles and armbands when swimming, as well as when hunting or fighting each other. In some pictures, they are shown wearing curious half-skirts, tied around the waist and hanging down the back as far as the knees, but open at the front.

Grass skirts appear in a later phase, when their paintings had become more sophisticated along with their clothing. Sometimes the skirts extend all the way around the body,

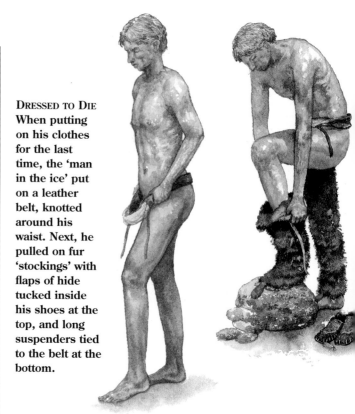

DRESSED TO DIE When putting on his clothes for the last time, the 'man in the ice' put on a leather belt, knotted around his waist. Next, he pulled on fur 'stockings' with flaps of hide tucked inside his shoes at the top, and long suspenders tied to the belt at the bottom.

but at other times they hang down at the front and back only, leaving the sides of the thighs bare. There are caps worn in this phase too, along with the armbands. In a later phase still, there are simple tunics of what may be linen cloth, shown as white against the dark skins of the figures. Elaborate headgear also appears in this phase, anticipating the fashions and artistic styles of ancient Egypt – a culture to which the people of Tassili undoubtedly contributed.

THE MAN IN THE ICE

Finding actual examples of Stone Age clothing seemed an impossible dream to archaeologists until 1991, when the body of a Neolithic man, 5300 years old, was found, preserved by ice in a glacier in northern Italy. Everything that would normally have

BIG BEAUTY Ice Age carvers admired shapely women, like this figure from Willendorf.

SIMULTANEOUS SERENDIPITY

The technique used to make the grass cape worn by the 5300-year-old man from the Alpine glacier was also developed quite independently in ancient Peru, as long as 10 000 years ago. Spinning and weaving were also invented independently in other parts of the world.

The loincloth (left) was next: a long piece of leather tucked into the belt at the back, brought forward between the legs, and pulled through the belt at the front. The spare length hung down to the man's knees, forming an apron. There was a short-sleeved tunic of fur and a grass cape on top.

been destroyed by scavengers, decay, wind and time – skin, eyes and clothing – had been preserved by the ice. Although the clothing was tattered, it could be pieced together with careful detective work, and the man's outfit reconstructed.

The outermost garments consisted of a conical fur cap tied with leather thongs beneath the chin, and a knee-length cape made of grass. This cape was made from sturdy, but flexible, grass stems that hung vertically, loosely linked together with horizontal strands of grass that were threaded through the vertical fibres. This strange garment was undoubtedly a primitive raincoat, with the smooth stems repelling rainwater, and channelling it downwards away from the other clothing. Such grass capes were still worn by peasants in northern Italy as recently as the 18th century.

All the remaining clothing was made of leather or fur, although the hairs had rubbed off from much of the fur, making it look rather like leather. Immediately beneath the grass cape was a knee-length tunic made of black and brown rectangles of fur, sewn together in a striped pattern. The man's legs were protected from the cold by deerskin leggings – a furry tube for each leg, held up by fur straps that were knotted to a leather belt. At the ankle, long flaps of

fur were sewn onto the leggings, which could be slipped inside the man's shoes to prevent the leggings from riding up.

Between the leggings and the tunic, the man wore a long loincloth of thin, soft leather. This cloth was looped through his belt at the back, brought forward between his legs, and then looped through his belt at the front, leaving enough leather to hang down in an apron to his knees.

Lastly, the man wore shoes of sturdy leather, probably from a cow, with an oval piece of leather forming the sole of each shoe. Above this, enclosing the foot, was a net made from grass-fibre cord, inside which the man had packed a thick wad of grass to keep in the heat. Covering the net and the grass stuffing was a fur upper, also sewn to the leather sole. The upper part of the shoe extended as far as the ankle. The shoes were tied around the ankles with grass cords, and two leather straps were knotted around the foot itself, partly to hold the shoes on, but also to give the wearer a better grip on any icy surfaces.

The sewing of the man's garments was neat and tight, most seams being joined with fine threads made from animal sinews. The garments were obviously not new, and some seams had broken open and needed repairs, particularly on the tunic.

The mending varied greatly in quality. In some places, it was the work of an expert, using thread made from hairs twisted with plant fibres. Other repairs were clumsily done with thick grass twine. The man had clearly not made his own clothing. Someone far more skilled had sewn the garments originally, but he was sometimes forced to mend tears for himself.

At first sight, the ancient fur and leather seemed to have been tanned by soaking in tannin-rich water, made by boiling up tree bark. But chemical analysis and microscopic examination showed this assumption to be incorrect. In fact, the clothes had been tanned using a more simple and primitive method: simply by smoking them over a fire. This technique prevents decomposition, but results in a stiff and unyielding product that would be far from comfortable to wear. To soften it, the smoked hide can be rubbed with grease, allowed to dry out again, and then softened by rubbing or even by chewing. It seems that the garments from the glacier had been prepared in this way.

The many hours of toil involved in making these clothes is difficult for us to imagine. Each skin had first to be cut from the flesh of the animal, scraped

FORERUNNER OF FABRIC **The idea of weaving cloth probably followed from experiments in cordwork and basketry. This example of woven cord comes from Peru.**

clean, and pegged to a wooden frame that would prevent it from shrinking and curling up as it was smoked and dried. Pieces would then be cut from the pelts, using sharp flint blades. Each item used in the preparation of the skins had also to be made from scratch: the wooden pegs and frame for staking out the skin, the stone scrapers for cleaning it of fat and flesh, the flint blades for cutting out the pattern, the sharp flint borers that made holes, the needles, and finally the thread itself. Flint blades would be blunted by the tough work of cutting thick hide, and new ones would have been made.

Even the very earliest and crudest clothing must have been time-consuming to make. It seems likely that these first clothes were simply hides and fur pelts, lashed about the body with rawhide thongs or animal sinews. Perhaps a hole was cut in a large pelt so that it could be placed over the head and anchored by the wearer's neck, before being fastened about the waist with a rough thong. The legs may have been kept warm by smaller pelts tied around them. Clothing such as this was probably worn by Neanderthals and by the earlier hominids as they moved out of Africa and into Europe for the first time. These people migrated into cold northerly

THE SILKWORM'S FIBRE

IN THE FAR EAST, a unique fibre was discovered. This was silk, a strong protein thread made by the caterpillar of a moth and wound around itself as a cocoon. One great advantage of silk is that it comes in a thread up to a mile long, and is then unwound from the cocoon, with no need for any spinning. Silk cloth was probably first woven about 5700 years ago. It became one of the most valued fabrics in the world and was later traded between the Far East and advanced civilisations such as Mesopotamia.

SHEEP AND WOOL IN PREHISTORIC TIMES

SHEEP were domesticated in the Middle East approximately 9000 years ago. These animals were kept for their meat, and had the coat of wild sheep – an outer layer of waterproof guard hairs, known as kemps, with just a thin layer of wool beneath.

At some stage, farmers must have realised the potential value of this wool, and began collecting it when the sheep moulted in the spring. In time, the farmers began to look for a thicker, woollier coat when choosing sheep from which to breed, and eventually sheep lost

SHEEPISH SURVIVORS Soay sheep resemble prehistoric breeds.

their kemps altogether, and were clothed only in a soft fleece. This process took thousands of years to develop, and it was only from 5000 years ago that archaeologists find

any evidence of wool being made into fabric.

The tradition of plucking the sheep as they moult probably persisted as the main method of wool collection until the Iron Age, when shears were invented. Even as late as the 19th century, Shetland islanders in the far north of Scotland plucked the wool from their sheep, rather than shearing them. Elsewhere in the world, the introduction of shearing brought an end to plucking wool, since sheep which are habitually shorn no longer moult in the spring.

latitudes, and it is hard to believe that they could have survived without some form of clothing.

One of the first woven textiles was linen, made from the long sturdy fibres that are found in the stem of flax, a blue-flowered plant that grows wild in many parts of Europe. The earliest evidence of linen cloth is some 8000 years old and comes from the Neolithic farming village of Çatal Hüyük in what is now Turkey.

THE FIRST TEXTILES

Long before that, flax fibres were probably used for making cord and rope, and it was a straightforward development to attempt to turn them into a material suitable for clothing. Because the flax fibres are so long, relatively little spinning is involved, and so the main labour with linen lies firstly in extracting the fibres – a tedious business in which the plant stems are soaked, fermented, beaten with wooden implements, soaked and beaten again – and secondly in weaving the cloth.

In the case of wool, cotton, alpaca and the many other yarns that were devised worldwide, spinning was a major task. The fibres of most of these materials were short, and to make them into thread it was necessary to twist them together using a handheld spindle – spinning wheels were a much later invention. This is monotonous work, although a skilled spinner can practise the craft while doing a whole range of other things – such as talking, storytelling,

watching over children, or tending herds of animals.

Weaving was a different matter, for it required specialised equipment that could not be carried around easily, and demanded careful attention at every moment. Looms were made from wood, with stone or pottery being used to weight the threads, and combs of bone to pack down the newly woven strands. The loom might stand upright from the floor, supported by wooden posts, or lie horizontally, raised off the ground a little way by wooden pegs. There were also semiportable devices known as backstrap looms (because one of the loom bars is attached to a belt which passes around the weaver's waist, enabling the weaver to adjust the tension of the warps as he leans forward or back). Prehistoric looms were often rather narrow, producing simple ribbons of cloth. In order to make these into garments, many strips would be sewn together.

ANCIENT EXPERIMENTS

The creative possibilities of weaving were explored at an early stage, and it was discovered that, by alternating different colours on the threads, striped, check or plaid patterns could be produced. In a peat bog in Denmark, the body of a young girl, dating from the Iron Age, was found with a band of striped cloth, in red, yellow and brown, tied over her eyes. In life, this pretty fabric had no doubt served as a headband, but the girl had been killed, either as a sacrifice or a punishment, and her colourful

since the individual hairs are covered with microscopic scales which can interlock and hold the hairs together. The tendency of wool to shrink when overheated helps the binding process.

To make felt, the loose wool fibres were spread out on the floor in a thick layer. Hot water was poured onto it and, when it had cooled sufficiently, the wool was trampled underfoot to compress it into a tough and flexible sheet of felt.

Felt-making is also a useful method for very short hairs such as those from a rabbit, which are difficult to spin into thread. For such hairs, some kind of gluey binding material is needed to hold the felt together. With the right combination of heat, pressure and binding agents, this can produce a relatively strong and durable fabric. Felt was particularly valued by nomadic herding people, like the Scythians, who used it for making boots, hats and tents.

CLEVER COLOURS

Dyeing fabric to produce colourful clothing was also a valued skill among prehistoric people. Certain plants, such as dyer's greenwood, weld and bog myrtle, could produce a yellow colour, while the leaves of indigo and woad gave a strong dark blue. Roots of madder grass were used for red in northern Europe, but in South America the blood of the cochineal bug, which fed on the juices of the prickly pear plant, was employed as a brilliant scarlet dye. In Central Europe, a similar insect (now known as the Polish cochineal beetle) was used for red.

Lichens could turn fabric brown or purple, and purplish hues could also be obtained from plants such as lady's bedstraw. A knowledge of which dyes lasted and which faded quickly would have been handed down from one generation to the next.

Some of the most brightly coloured and sumptuous cloths come from the prehistoric era in Peru. The forerunners of Peruvian textiles are more than 10 500 years

ROOTS OF THE LOOM The vertical loom was used by many prehistoric communities; in principle, it is the same as modern hand-weaving looms.

headband used to blindfold her before her death.

Prehistoric people carried out an impressive range of experiments with different fibres in their efforts to find the best possible fabrics. As well as the wool of sheep, there were experiments with hair from goats, camels, dogs, cows, horses, beavers and rabbits. In the Americas, the hair of vicunas, guanacos and buffaloes was also used. Even human hair was spun and woven into cloth in the New World. Fibres from nettles, hemp, yucca leaves, and half a dozen other more obscure plants were employed at one time or another. Asbestos was dug, and its fibres were made into cloth in one part of Eurasia, and the long anchoring threads from a type of shellfish, similar to a mussel, were woven into a fine shimmering cloth in some regions of the Mediterranean. This practice survived into historic times, and the 'cloth of gold' of Greek legend was probably woven from these shellfish.

There were simpler methods than weaving, of which the least demanding was to make a felt material. Sheep's wool was employed,

LOSING THE THREAD A ball of thread, lost or discarded in France over 5000 years ago, represented hours of wasted plucking and spinning.

EXTRAVAGANT TEXTILES In prehistoric Peru, textile weaving and embroidery reached extraordinary heights.

old, and consist of pouches and small baskets made from grass stems and other plant fibres, which were twisted and looped together. The huge gaps in the archaeological record, created by the perishable nature of cloth, make it difficult to know how quickly real textiles developed from these early experiments, but by 5000 years ago textiles were being made from twined yarn, often a combination of cotton and the long fibres from plant stems.

Even at this early stage, there were designs being

MINIATURE MASTERPIECE This woven ornament illustrates the virtuosity of prehistoric Peruvian weavers. Their skills remain unmatched even today.

woven into the cloth, including illustrations of snakes, condors and people. Materials for burial wrappings were already being woven at this early date, and by 3400 years ago the Peruvian textile makers had advanced to cotton tapestries.

PREHISTORIC PERU

Embroidery became a major art form at Paracas, situated in the Peruvian coastal desert, where caves have yielded embroidered mantles with matching tunics, loincloths and headbands, all immaculately preserved by the extraordinary dryness of the desert air. These fabrics, produced between 2600 and 2170 years ago, were richly decorated with human and mythological figures. In some examples,

the style followed the traditional geometric patterns and squared-off figure outlines seen in other South American fabrics, while in other Paracas embroideries there is a greater fluidity and freedom of expression, with curved lines giving an unusual liveliness to the humans, gods and animals depicted. The woollen thread used for these embroideries was dyed in up to 18 different colours for a single mantle, with as many as 13 colours used for one figure alone.

Calculations of the time demanded by this embroidery show that it could have taken one person over ten years to produce a typical set of Paracas garments, assuming they worked for 35 hours each week. Similar amounts of labour were invested in mummies found elsewhere in Peru, dating from about 2000 years ago. They were bundled up in woven cloth padded out with leaves and raw cotton. Bags containing coca leaves and plant seeds hung from belts around the bundle, while intricate cords and braids lashed everything together. The total length of cloth used in a typical bundle was 200 ft (60 m), requiring a spinning time of over 4000 hours. This alone would have taken a single worker

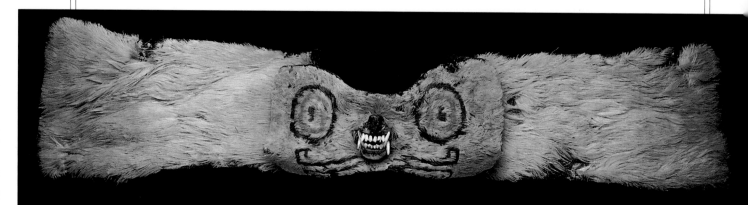

COLOURS FROM THE FOREST The brilliant feathers of macaw parrots, hunted in rain forests far away and brought over the Andes by traders, give colour to this Peruvian headband.

SPECTACULAR SHROUD The body was placed in the funerary basket (above), with a gourd bowl. Reeds were placed over the body and brightly coloured cloths were then wrapped around it (right).

two and a half years of full time work. Such textiles were made as offerings for the dead, as were some of the clothes found in burials. These seem to have been made exclusively for the dead because they have only been discovered at funeral sites. The additional labour of spinning and weaving for the living must have made this a major occupation of the prehistoric Peruvians.

Their obsession with producing fine fabrics was extraordinary. As well as embroidery, they created a range of complex weaving techniques, including tapestry weaving, in which pictures were built up by adding floating crosswise threads to the basic weave. Pile weaving, producing a carpet-like effect, was also practised for items such as caps. Other sophisticated techniques included making double cloth or even triple cloth, where two or three layers were made simultaneously and linked together during the weaving to give a thick warm fabric. Among the many decorative techniques, these prehistoric people developed painting on cloth, and printing using a carved pattern on a gourd.

One extraordinarily complex form of decoration involved weaving several separate square areas of fabric on a loom, joined only by the structural threads known as the warp. Once the squares had been woven, the whole thing was removed from the loom and each square dyed separately. The dying process involved two or more colours to produce a

pattern on each square. The half-finished fabric was then returned to the loom, and the gaps filled in with further weaving.

Compared with this time-consuming obsession with cloth-making techniques, the Peruvians, for the most part, showed little interest in tailoring their garments. Rectangular pieces of cloth would be joined leaving a slit for the neck, in the style of a poncho, but little or no attempt was made to shape the garments to the human frame. Mantles were simply rectangles of cloth draped around the shoulder. Loincloths consisted of a rectangular apron tied around the waist, with a long band of cloth then looped between the legs. Skirts and tunics for women were equally simple in their construction.

Clothing from Danish peat bogs often shows a similar indifference to tailoring. A woman's dress may have consisted of nothing more than a voluminous tube of woven woollen cloth fixed with a brooch above each shoulder. The top end of the cloth tube was generously folded outwards before being pinned, so that the flaps fell over the woman's chest and back. These ample folds of fabric created a makeshift sleeve that partially enclosed her upper arms, but also left thick folds of cloth underneath her arms, which must have been inconvenient. Such simplicity is a further indication that personal ornamentation and weaving were more sophisticated in prehistoric times than tailoring itself.

VENTURING INTO THE UNKNOWN

Tens of thousands of years before Europeans first began to explore the oceans,

prehistoric people were making epic overland treks across the Americas – and

voyaging hundreds of miles across the Pacific without any navigational instruments.

FOR most people today, it would be unthinkable to set off into the unknown without a map, and with no idea of what lay ahead, simply trusting that food and water would be found, and that there would be somewhere to shelter when night fell. Yet this apparently reckless activity was commonplace for prehistoric people.

It was with such faith in the land, and in their own mastery of it, that early hominids set out from their homelands in Africa over a million years ago and spread northwards, each generation travelling a few miles, then settling for a while. Generation by generation, they moved outwards and onwards, eventually leaving Africa and venturing into Europe and Asia. For hundreds of thousands of years, there was an endless flow of our human ancestors back and forth across Eurasia. Yet large parts of the world remained unexplored. Some 40 000 years ago the vast wildernesses of North and South America were probably still uninhabited. The colonisation of Australia was just beginning, but human feet had yet to tread the islands of Micronesia and Polynesia. New Zealand, too, was unpopulated and would remain so for a very long time.

WALKING ON WATER

During the ice ages, the sea level dropped so low that many journeys which would require a sea crossing today could be made on foot. Prehistoric people could have walked from northern Europe into Britain and from India to Sri Lanka. There were land bridges from mainland east Asia across to Japan, and it was possible to walk from the South-east Asian mainland south to Sumatra, across to Borneo and on to the Philippines.

The falling sea levels of the ice ages created the supercontinent of Sahul, encompassing Australia, New Guinea and Tasmania, together with large areas of land that are now seabed. It was to this great continent that the first Australians, the ancestors of present-day Australian Aboriginal people, travelled.

THE FIRST AUSTRALIANS

They came from South-east Asia, probably via the island of Timor, or from the Celebes and Moluccas, farther to the north. Whichever route was used, an unbroken sea journey of 38 miles (60 km) or more was required for the last stage of this voyage. These colonisers arrived in Australasia at least 50 000 years ago, and perhaps even earlier.

What kind of boat was used to reach Australasia remains a mystery. At such an early date, it was probably a simple, crudely made craft, perhaps nothing more than a raft lashed together from logs or bamboo. It would not have been particularly sturdy, and must have survived the crossing through sheer luck. Sahul could not be seen, even from the highest point of Timor, so the colonists set out without knowing if there would be land over the horizon. However, they had with them the makings of a new life: they probably carried stone tools and bamboo vessels holding drinking water, and there must have been women on board, as well as men, to start a new

TRAVELLING HOPEFULLY A Pacific island shimmers on the horizon, perhaps uninhabitable, perhaps a potential paradise. The human urge to find out led prehistoric people to the far corners of the Earth.

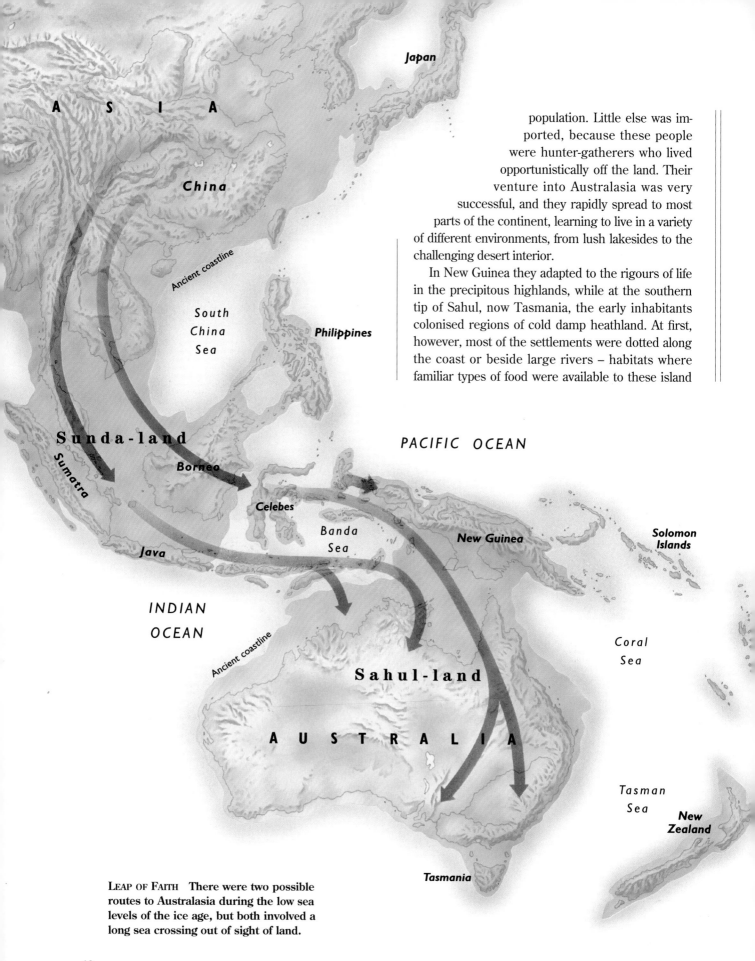

Japan

A S I A

China

Ancient coastline

South
China
Sea

Philippines

Sunda-land

Sumatra

Borneo

Java

Celebes

INDIAN
OCEAN

Ancient coastline

Banda
Sea

PACIFIC OCEAN

New Guinea

Solomon
Islands

Coral
Sea

S a h u l - l a n d

A U S T R A L I A

Tasman
Sea

New
Zealand

Tasmania

population. Little else was imported, because these people
were hunter-gatherers who lived
opportunistically off the land. Their
venture into Australasia was very
successful, and they rapidly spread to most
parts of the continent, learning to live in a variety
of different environments, from lush lakesides to the
challenging desert interior.

In New Guinea they adapted to the rigours of life
in the precipitous highlands, while at the southern
tip of Sahul, now Tasmania, the early inhabitants
colonised regions of cold damp heathland. At first,
however, most of the settlements were dotted along
the coast or beside large rivers – habitats where
familiar types of food were available to these island

LEAP OF FAITH There were two possible
routes to Australasia during the low sea
levels of the ice age, but both involved a
long sea crossing out of sight of land.

people. Only later did they conquer the more alien types of environment.

There may well have been several influxes of people into Australasia from South-east Asia. Some archaeologists characterised the earliest Australians as being more lightly built than modern Aborigines, with less distinctive facial features, as shown by finds from Lake Mungo in what is now New South Wales, occupied over 30 000 years ago. Other immigrants from Asia may have introduced the heavy brow ridges and facial features characteristic of modern Aborigines. Some late arrivals, who reached Australia only 4000 years ago, brought with them domestic dogs which escaped to become the wild dingoes of modern Australia.

ANCIENT TRADITIONS When this rock painting was made by Aborigines 6500 years ago, their ancestors had inhabited Australia for about 43 500 years.

At the close of the last ice age, some 10 000 years ago, sea levels rose again, cutting off New Guinea and Tasmania from the Australian continent. From then on, the isolation of the Aborigines increased, although finds from the northern coasts show that they were visited, thousands of years later, by sea-cucumber gatherers from Sulawesi.

THE PEOPLING OF THE AMERICAS

Most archaeologists agree that humankind did not penetrate the New World until about 15 000 years ago. A minority view, based on a few scattered sites, favours earlier arrivals, perhaps as ancient as 40 000 years ago. It is beyond dispute, however, that the major colonisation of the Americas occurred in a substantial wave just over 11 000 years ago, by hunter-gatherers known as the 'Clovis people'.

The forerunners of the Clovis people came from the far north of Asia, and they came on foot. This migration occurred during the last ice age, when sea levels had fallen so much that the area between Siberia and Alaska, now covered by the seas of the Bering Strait, was dry land. Archaeologists refer to this lost land as Beringia.

Beringia may have been a dismal unproductive tundra landscape, or a slightly more hospitable zone of steppe grassland – opinions differ – but there is no doubt that it was piercingly cold, lying so close to the Arctic ice sheet. Large herds of cold-loving mammals, such as woolly mammoths, reindeer and bison, roamed these parts and drew hunters into the area in search of food.

It is believed that people lived in Beringia from about 18 000 years ago, without venturing very far to the east. They may have remained there until the ice age came to an end and rising sea levels flooded Beringia, forcing them to move back into Asia or southwards into North America. Some of them decided to move south, following the herds of game. The farther south they went, the better things got. There were warmer climates, abundant grasslands, and huge herds of bison and mammoth to hunt, including species of mammoth that they had never seen before – all 'easy game', unaccustomed to the wiles of human predators.

It was in this welcoming environment that the Clovis culture emerged 11 200 years ago. Clovis people made large and neatly chipped stone spearheads which are found in archaeological sites right across the American continent. As well as big game, they hunted deer, rabbits and other small animals, and caught fish in the lakes and rivers.

Spreading ever southwards, their descendants moved into South America in a remarkably short space of time. Their waves of migration were accompanied by waves of extinction for many of the large mammals that they hunted, from mammoths and mastodons in North America to giant sloths in South America. Although hunting itself probably contributed to these extinctions, the more arid climate

SPEARHEADING AN INVASION Spearheads were typical of the Clovis people who colonised North America.

and changing vegetation that followed the end of the ice age may also have played a part.

The decline of the big game-herds spelled the end of the Clovis culture, but the people themselves survived, adapting to local conditions wherever they found themselves, and so becoming progressively more different, one tribe from another. Some became farmers, others remained as hunter-gatherers, while those on the northern Pacific coast developed into full-time salmon fishermen. Around these very different ways of life, distinctive customs, religious beliefs, forms of dress, housing and artistic styles developed, emphasising even more the differences between the tribes.

VOYAGES IN POLYNESIA

The last area of the world to be colonised by humankind was Polynesia. The move began when people from Indonesia and the Philippines moved southeastwards into central Melanesia, including the Solomon Islands and the Bismarck Archipelago. Exactly when this occurred is not clear; but from there, the colonists sailed eastwards in ocean-going canoes to explore and settle the deserted islands of the remote Pacific. This great migration began about 3500 years ago. Other migrants probably travelled from an area to the west of New Guinea and sailed towards the north-east to settle the islands known as Micronesia.

These were skilled seafarers. For almost 30 000 years, people had inhabited the string of tropical islands that stretch south-eastwards into the Pacific Ocean from New Guinea to the Solomon Islands – a maritime corridor where conditions are ideal for practising inter-island navigation. The islands can mostly be seen one from the other, making it unnecessary to sail beyond sight of land.

Fishing expeditions and trade between the islands of central Melanesia had honed the maritime skills and boat-building techniques of the people who lived there. Techniques of safe navigation had been learned during the long interval – over 25 000 years – between the arrival of humanity in Melanesia and their migration eastwards, first towards Fiji, Tonga and Samoa, and then on to the far-flung islands of Polynesia, ultimately reaching Hawaii and Easter Island.

Their early migrations took them into the teeth of

trade winds which blow westwards in this part of the Pacific. Archaeologists used to puzzle over the incongruity of prehistoric people migrating against the prevailing wind, since they believed that exploration and discovery must have been due to journeys that had gone awry: boats being blown off course and then luckily striking new lands. It fitted with a notion of prehistoric people as naive, unskilful opportunists.

Modern research suggests the exact opposite. It seems that the Polynesian colonisers of 3500 years ago were expert sailors, who had learned that the safest way to travel was to seize those rare opportunities when the trade winds drop and then sail in an easterly direction, since the winds would inevitably rouse themselves once more and blow the boats back home. Trade winds, far from being a barrier to eastward migration, were a safety net – a dependable force that would usually bring sailors back to base, making excursions into the open ocean less hazardous.

The people who set off so confidently into the great blue void of the Pacific Ocean belonged to a cultural group that modern archaeologists call Lapita. A particular kind of pottery characterises Lapita, and was carried eastwards from Melanesia in the canoes of the early colonists. Lapita pottery was made without a wheel, being built up of coils and slabs. If there was any decoration at all, this was impressed onto the half-hardened clay to produce fine lines and rows of dots. The process was repeated to make geometric patterns, or to show symbols and stylised faces.

As well as the pottery, Lapita peoples possessed other characteristic items, such as bracelets and arm-rings made of shell, and fish-hooks carved from pearl shell. Although finds of the pottery itself do not

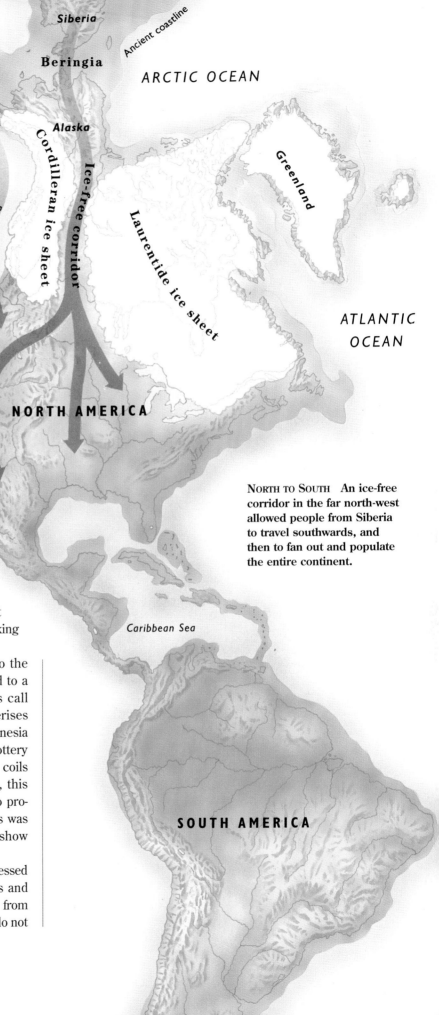

NORTH TO SOUTH An ice-free corridor in the far north-west allowed people from Siberia to travel southwards, and then to fan out and populate the entire continent.

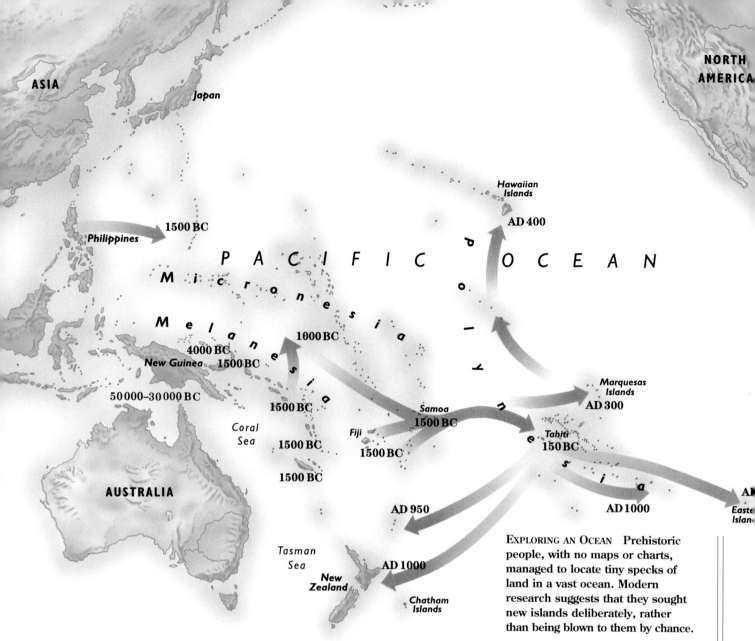

ASIA

Japan

NORTH
AMERICA

PACIFIC OCEAN

Philippines **1500 BC**

Hawaiian
Islands

AD 400

M i c r o n e s i a

M e l a n e s i a

1000 BC

4000 BC
New Guinea **1500 BC**

50 000–30 000 BC

Coral
Sea

1500 BC

1500 BC

Fiji

Samoa
1500 BC

1500 BC

1500 BC

AUSTRALIA

1500 BC

P
o
l
y
n
e
s
i
a

Marquesas
Islands
AD 300

Tahiti
150 BC

AD 950

AD 1000

AD 1000

Tasman
Sea

New
Zealand

Chatham
Islands

Easte
Islan

EXPLORING AN OCEAN Prehistoric
people, with no maps or charts,
managed to locate tiny specks of
land in a vast ocean. Modern
research suggests that they sought
new islands deliberately, rather
than being blown to them by chance.

extend right into Polynesia, the distinctive collection
of other artefacts has allowed archaeologists to plot
the expansion of the Lapita groups.

They moved with surprising rapidity, which suggests that systematic exploration of the ocean for
new islands was part of their way of life, and that
their culture imbued them with a powerful urge to
expand and colonise. There were probably two
kinds of journey: exploratory and colonising. On the
exploratory trips, the canoes carried enough food
and water to keep the explorers alive for several
weeks. This was the first stage. Once a new island
had been discovered, it would probably be visited
several times to ensure its suitability and to confirm
the ocean route required to reach it reliably and, just
as importantly, to return safely each time.

Eventually, a party of colonists would embark on
a completely different kind of voyage. Women, and
possibly children, would travel in the canoes at this
stage. According to modern computer simulations,
at least four or five adults would be needed to set up
a viable new colony, and there were probably more
in most cases. They took with them domesticated
plants such as yams, taro, breadfruit and bananas.
Coconuts might be included unless there were trees
there already, growing wild.

Animals were also transported, including chickens, pigs and possibly dogs. Rats often travelled in
the canoes, either as unwanted pests or, tolerated
perhaps, as a source of meat, for the islanders
would happily catch and cook these rodents. As
well as pots and other equipment, the colonists

NAVIGATING BY NIGHT

PRESENT-DAY POLYNESIAN navigators can sense a coral reef, way below the ocean surface, and so detect its presence at night.

Phosphorescence – a sparkling light in the darkened water that is generated by microscopic marine animals – occurs widely in tropical seas, but a particular kind of phosphorescence can, to an expert eye, indicate the presence of a reef beneath the surface, and show that an island lies ahead. Quite apart from these abilities, traditional Polynesian navigators today often know where they are in a seemingly featureless ocean beneath a cloudy sky.

would take raw material for making equipment in the future, such as obsidian, a volcanic glass that is chipped to form sharp cutting tools. There would be some food, stored in baskets, to sustain them through the early months, although they would also rely on fish, sea birds, eggs, and the other abundant, easily plundered foods of the uninhabited island.

OCEAN PIONEERS

The new arrivals were not totally alone, since voyages to and from their home island occurred regularly. The distribution of obsidian shows that trade and contact between the islands were intensive. Knowledge of life in some parts of Micronesia today may be relevant to understanding ancient Polynesia. Here there are many small, ecologically vulnerable islands, whose low-lying crop gardens can be utterly destroyed by a cyclone and flooded with salt water so that they take years to recover fully. These fragile islands are still linked by constant voyaging and by networks of mutual support, allowing people to survive such crises by evacuating the island and then returning later, when conditions permit.

In Micronesia, people as well as goods travel back and forth across the sea, as men take wives from distantly related families on another island, or prospective husbands travel to the island of their bride to fulfil an arranged marriage. Relatives visit each other and children may be adopted by kin from another island, adding to the network of relationship and mutual obligation that holds people together and aids survival. It may have been the same in ancient Polynesia, as small pioneer communities struggled to establish a viable way of life on their newly colonised islands.

Once the pioneer colony on a new Polynesian island had firmly taken root and numbers had built up over the generations, a new bout of exploration and colonisation would begin. In this way, the Lapita culture, having reached Fiji by about 3000 years ago, moved on to the Cook Islands and the Society Islands in the central Pacific by about 2000 years ago.

From there, the colonists ventured northwards, sailing bravely across the prevailing winds – a dangerous enterprise since they could not cruise home on the trade winds. Nevertheless they survived, and had settled Hawaii by about 1500 years ago. The epic journey to Easter Island in the far distant east of the Pacific was also completed by about AD 500.

The journey south-westwards from Polynesia to New Zealand occurred surprisingly late, about 1000 years ago, and the last islands to be settled, the Chatham Islands to the east of New Zealand, were

PACIFIC POTS Not all Lapita pottery was as heavily decorated as these fragments of 3000-year-old pots from the Santa Cruz islands.

not colonised until about 500 years ago.

The prehistoric sailors of the Pacific developed a truly astonishing expertise in navigation, and a remarkable knowledge of the geography of their ocean. Almost unbelievably, they did it without a compass or other instrument of navigation and, as far as we know, without maps or charts – indeed, with no form of written record whatsoever. They might measure the angle of a star by holding out a splayed hand at arm's length, or perhaps use a piece of twine with a stone tied to one end to give an accurate vertical line, but nothing more.

By the 19th century, Micronesian navigators were using simple model-like 'charts', made up of a framework of wood strips or plant stems which indicated the currents and swells, and with cowrie shells attached to the framework to indicate islands. There is no evidence of anything like this from Polynesia, and the Micronesian charts could have been a late acquisition, inspired by Western maps.

For the ancient Lapita colonisers, it seems that routes across the great unmarked spaces of the ocean were memorised by expert navigators, who probably used chants and other mnemonic devices to help them. Movements of the stars and sun, in all their complexity, were also memorised.

Other means of finding the way were also committed to memory and passed down from generation to generation. These included the characteristic pattern of waves and swells in different parts of the ocean; the colour of a distant coral atoll reflected in the clouds, and therefore visible long before the island itself rose above the horizon; the roosting habits of sea birds, such as terns and noddies, whose flight could indicate the direction of land; and hundreds of other small signs that might mean the difference between survival and death in those precarious waters.

Navigators had to summon up all this memorised

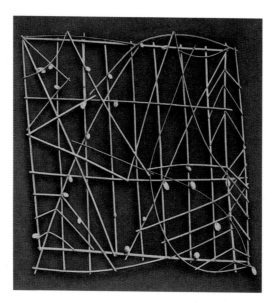

MICRONESIAN MAP   Micronesian islanders made navigation charts; the rods indicate currents, while the shells are islands.

knowledge, and then to perform the complex mental computations that were needed to apply it to a particular situation, even if they were exhausted, faint with hunger or thirst, and soaked to the skin by a tropical storm. Lives depended on such mental abilities.

A few traditional Polynesian navigators still practise their skills, and studies of them reveal a surprising approach to voyaging. Rather than having a mental map of the ocean, in the Western way, some Polynesians work on the notion of the canoe as a fixed point, around which stars, water and islands move. The journey is divided into a notional series of blocks, with each segment having to be completed before the next can begin. It is a complex idea so alien to our own way of thinking that we find it difficult to comprehend, yet it works: such methods took the prehistoric voyagers 6250 miles (10 000 km) across the sea, from Melanesia to Easter Island.

EAST TO AMERICA

Polynesian seafarers probably went farther still and may even have reached the South American mainland. Evidence for this idea lies in the fact that sweet potatoes, originally a South American crop, are known to have been well established in places such as New Guinea at least 5000 to 4000 years ago. They were grown all across Polynesia and as far south as New Zealand during the later phases of Pacific prehistory, which indicates the likelihood of some form of contact between South America and the Pacific islands. It seems that the Polynesians may have landed by canoe on the western shores of South America and exchanged goods for sweet potatoes with the coastal Indians. How amazed they must have been at finding a land so large they could not sail around it. Whether prehistoric South Americans made the trip in the opposite direction, independently of this, is an open question. They certainly

TREES TO TRAVEL IN　　**A process of repeated burning and scraping turns a tree trunk into an ocean-going canoe.**

reached the Galápagos Islands, but there is no evidence that they went farther.

It is suspected that the Polynesian adventurers reached South America between about 1000 and 1500 years ago. This may have been an isolated event, and there was certainly very little contact, even if such journeys were carried out more than once. This is shown by the limited genetic variation among sweet potatoes grown in the Pacific.

Lapita culture declined almost as rapidly as it had grown. The typical pottery of Lapita fell out of use before the colonisers had travelled far beyond Samoa and Tonga. In its place, traditional coconut shells and gourds acted as perfect lightweight

DISTANT GODS On Easter Island, the most far-flung outpost of Pacific colonisation, stone statues of the gods tower over the deforested terrain.

ancient occupation. Far larger than most of these ghost islands but at the farthest edge of Polynesia, Easter Island was probably isolated soon after it was colonised. The human population flourished there initially, developing an extraordinary culture which raised more than 600 massive stone statues on the hillsides.

Felling the trees of Easter Island eroded the soil, and as a result the environment deteriorated rapidly. A lack of timber made it impossible for the survivors to build canoes and therefore escape their impoverished island, and their culture declined along with their food supply. Although Easter Island was still inhabited when it was finally discovered by European ships in the 18th century, it seems likely that it would have become uninhabited if left to itself, unsupported by trade or contact with other parts of Polynesia.

When New Zealand was colonised by the Polynesians about 500 years ago, they had to adapt to a new terrain and a temperate climate that is fundamentally unsuited to tropical plants such as bananas, breadfruit, coconuts and yams.

THE ORIGINAL MAORIS

The survival of the Maoris depended, at least in part, on plants which they found in their new homeland. These included roots of bracken fern, so coarse that it wore people's teeth down to mere stumps, bullrush roots, berries, and the buds of the cabbage tree (a type of palm tree). Early Maoris had brought dogs with them, and probably used these for food, as was common throughout Polynesia.

They had no need of chickens, since the new land boasted its own 'giant chickens' in the form of massive flightless birds that the Maoris named moas. The largest species stood 6 ft (1.8 m) tall but it was a harmless herbivore, unused to predators,

containers. At a later stage, regular travel and trade between the islands also declined, and the individual islands or island groups became increasingly isolated. For some islands – especially the smaller ones, or those without good fishing, fertile soil or adequate water – the decline in trade and contact spelled the end for human occupation. There are more than 25 of these ghostly, uninhabited islands scattered across the Pacific, each with traces of

TRACKS OF TIME

Some of the tracks and paths established in prehistoric times are still in use today. Mountain passes in the Alps of Europe were explored by prehistoric travellers, who found the safest routes by trial and error. The same is true of paths on drier ground that weave between the marshlands of Denmark. These ancient routes are still re-traced by modern feet.

TRACKS ACROSS THE MARSHLANDS OF SOMERSET

SEVEN thousand years ago a large area of south-west England, now known as the Somerset Levels, was covered by the sea. When the sea level fell, over 5500 years ago, the salty mud was slowly colonised by tall waving reeds and other marsh plants. To the prehistoric farmers who lived on the higher land north and south of the marsh, this was a wilderness of water-logged ground and meandering streams. Gradually, they found ways through the marsh, as they went in search of birds such as bitterns, herons and ducks, which made good eating.

They established routes through the marsh, and eventually decided to improve the main path by putting a wooden trackway along it. Over 5000 years ago, they built the Sweet Track, an ambitious board-walk made entirely of wood, which has survived to be excavated by archaeologists. Great time and effort were required to fell the wood used for making the track, which seems to have been the work of a community of Neolithic farmers.

In advance of the track itself, they built a rough pathway of planks to provide a dry footing from which they could work. The permanent path they made was a sturdy construction based on pairs of pegs set diagonally, which supported thick branches and, above these, planks that formed the surface of the track.

Sweet Track is re-markably straight, and survived well for about a decade – with occasional repairs, particularly in wetter areas where the wood was more prone to rot, or tended to be swept away by the winter rains. After the Sweet Track fell into disuse, no fur-ther wooden tracks were built for about 1000 years, as far as we know. Between 4500 and 3000 years ago, at least four more tracks were made. Three of these were flimsy affairs, using nothing more than hurdles woven from fine hazel stems, but one was of a similar size to the Sweet Track.

WELL-WORN ROUTE The Sweet Track, built more than 5000 years ago in the marshes of Somerset, has been reduced to a jumble of sodden timbers by the passage of time.

and therefore easily felled by stone-tipped spears. Other wild animals that could be used for food included kiwis and parrots, crayfish, eels, seals and seabirds. With careful cultivation techniques, yams, taro and gourds could be grown in the warmer zones of North Island, and the same proved true of the sweet potato when this was introduced to New Zealand about 600 years ago.

The last lands to be colonised by prehistoric people were the Chatham Islands, which lie to the east of New Zealand. Although the colonising Maoris probably set out with crops, intent on farming their new home, the cool climate and difficult terrain of the Chatham Islands forced them to abandon agri-culture and to live as hunter-gatherers.

Fish, shellfish and other coastal resources were the mainstay of their existence, and the only animals they brought with them from New Zealand were rats. It seems that there was little contact between New Zealand and the Chatham Islands: by the 18th century, their inhabitants did not even know of each other's existence.

THE FIRST HOUSES

The earliest evidence of habitation comes from southern France

and dates back some 300 000 years. With these first huts came the notion that humans

might create their own environment – an artificial world of warmth and safety.

BEFORE LEAVING their camp site, they collect up their belongings, their stone tools and wooden digging sticks. Women tie the smallest children to their sides in slings of animal hide. Finally, all is ready and they leave: a group of nomadic hunter-gatherers on the move once again, in a scene that must have been re-enacted many times in the course of human prehistory.

Behind them is the temporary home which they had built three days earlier, using slender young branches hacked from nearby trees and propped up together to form a conical shelter. To stabilise the structure, they had scraped out some shallow holes in which the ends of the branches rested. But the hut was still rickety – so they had collected a few large stones and placed them against the most unstable branches. When this basic frame-work was secure, handfuls of dried grass were stuffed into the gaps in the outside. It was enough to keep the wind off them during their stay.

Two days after leaving their camp site, a storm loosens the structure and the long branches topple to the ground: soon afterwards, a herd of antelope pass through and scatter the branches further. Soil churned up by their hooves begins to fill the holes

dug for the uprights, and a dust storm completes the process. After a few months, the only remaining signs of the shelter are those large stones, five in all, that were used to stabilise the uprights.

The stones do not mark out a complete circle on the soil: two are together on one side; the other three are distributed around the vanished perimeter of the hut. Half a million years later, archaeologists examining the site puzzle over these five stones. One sees a circle marked out by the stones and be-lieves that they were placed there deliberately, by the same hands that left a few cutting tools and some butchered antelope bones nearby. Another archaeologist points to similar stones scattered ran-domly over the ancient soil surface and suggests that the 'circle' is a chance formation.

VANISHED TRACES

Most of the earliest dwellings of our ancestors must have vanished in this way, scattered like dust, leaving no definite sign. This is why it is difficult to pinpoint the moment when our ancestors began to build homes for themselves.

LUNG DISEASE

Breathing the dust produced by flint can cause a lung disease known as silicosis, which can be fatal. Prehistoric people making tools would have been at risk from this, suffering symptoms such as shortness of breath. Knapping flint indoors was especially hazardous, but this would probably not have been recognised because the effects of flint dust appear slowly, as dust accumulates in the lungs. It takes at least a year, and usually a decade, for silicosis to become obvious.

INSTANT HOUSING One simple way to make a temporary hut is to cut down large branches or young sapling trees, and prop these together to form a conical shape. Leaves or grass are then used to fill in the gaps.

The earliest undisputed outlines of huts, found at Terra Amata in southern France, date from about 300 000 years ago. There are a succession of huts, built on a beach by hunter-gatherers who returned to the same spot every spring for about 20 years. The huts are up to 49 ft (15 m) long and 20 ft (6 m) wide, oval in shape, and supported by two or more stout poles set in a row down the long axis. The walls were made of slender branches about 3 in (7.5 cm) in diameter, set in the ground and then stabilised with stones around the outside.

ANCIENT TRADITIONS In parts of the world, including Australia, temporary huts are still made as they were hundreds of thousands of years ago.

59

This careful construction work suggests that hut-building may already have been an established practice, and archaeologists suspect that, long before Terra Amata, there must have been many much simpler man-made shelters. Some may have been little more than a row of sticks standing vertically in the ground to form a windbreak, or a rough 'lean-to' made by resting leafy branches against the low-sweeping bough of an ancient tree. Makeshift structures such as these have been described by anthropologists studying several groups of nomadic and seminomadic people.

The !Kung San of the Kalahari Desert are nomadic hunter-gatherers who build temporary accommodation for overnight stops during expeditions. Their approach may give some insight into the learning process of the earliest hut-builders, who inhabited a similar climate and landscape. Occasionally, to save time and effort at the end of a long day's hunting, the !Kung San use a large bush to form one side of the temporary hut – a 'living wall' that gives added solidity because the rest of the hut can be propped up against it.

Perhaps the earliest huts developed in this way: first as people took refuge from the wind in the lee of a bush; and then, as later generations realised that they could add branches from trees to improve a small or leafless bush. By a gradual process, they might have reached the point where the bush was only part of a comprehensive, all-round structure. From there, it was a small step to making the entire hut themselves.

This learning process continued throughout prehistory, as people migrated into new areas, and had to contend with different climates – often colder, wetter and windier – and with a different range of raw materials for building. The ice ages brought a special challenge, not just because the temperatures fell, but also because the forests died out over much of Europe, to be replaced by a thin vegetation of lichens and low-growing bushes. There was little wood to build with, in a world that had grown unbearably cold.

HARD TIMES

That our ancestors solved this problem, and flourished during the European ice ages is a testament to their extraordinary ingenuity and imagination in devising new forms of building. That same creativity allowed them to conquer a vast range of different conditions as they spread across the globe, always devising a satisfactory solution to the problem of where to live.

Their survival is also a testament to their tolerance of smoke, bad smells, poor light and draughts – their domestic environment was one that we would now find uninhabitable. It was thousands of years before the first chimney or stovepipe was invented, and throughout these years people simply built a hearth in the middle of their hut or tent, and made a hole in the roof directly above, through which smoke could escape. There is little doubt that its course skywards was a meandering one, and that the atmosphere within the dwelling was tough on the lungs.

THE PAST REVISITED Archaeologists have attempted to reconstruct the huts built at Terra Amata – this shows the basic framework.

KEEPING WARM AND SAFE

WE ARE SO USED to having a roof over our heads, particularly at night, that we would feel very insecure sleeping out in the open, especially with predatory animals roaming the land. We tend to take it for granted that our ancestors felt the same, and that building huts was therefore a logical step for humankind. In fact, unless there is a camp fire burning to keep predators away, the walls of a flimsy hut are more of a liability than an asset, preventing the occupants from keeping a lookout on all sides. Far from offering our earliest ancestors security, a hut would have made them a sitting target for marauders such as lions.

Our ancestors often made use of caves and overhanging rocks for shelter. In mild climates, their major attraction was that they required no building materials and little work, other than making a hearth and clearing away the debris of previous occupants, animal or human. A cave kept people dry during rainstorms, and gave some protection from the wind. Sometimes occupants of caves did try to improve their dwellings by

WINDOW ON A FROZEN WORLD This is the view from La Vache cave in France, which was inhabited during the Ice Age.

constructing a windbreak of branches across the cave entrance, or by narrowing the entrance with stone. In the hostile conditions of Ice Age Europe, more drastic improvements were needed to make the caves habitable. Huts were sometimes built within the caves, using either stones or a framework of wooden poles, covered perhaps

with animal skins. In a cave, known as La Grotte du Renne, at Arcy-sur-Cure in France, a hut was built of mammoth tusks, set in the ground to form an arch-like framework.

The first hut-dwellers would have found a camp fire essential for driving away nocturnal predators, and giving people the confidence to sleep the night within the blinkered confines of a hut. So it seems possible that, in the development of human skills, the domestication of fire preceded hut-building. Fire was also essential for cave-dwellers, to ward off animals such as hyenas and bears which use caves for their lairs, and to make caves themselves more habitable. Without fire, it is unlikely that anyone could have endured the cold and damp of northern caves, such as those near modern Beijing, at the site known as Zhoukoudian, where generation upon generation of our ancestors lived.

People lived and slept close together, and the natural smells of their bodies would have combined with those of home-tanned animal hides, rank furs, meat roasted on the fire, animal blood and grease dropped on the floor, bones being dried for toolmaking or fuel, and damp clothing drying out after a rainstorm. No doubt these people had a less judgmental attitude towards smells than we have, regarding a great variety of scents with impartial interest, in much the way that dogs do. The combined aromas of sweat, smoke and damp fur probably had familiar, homely connotations for them, and was comforting rather than offensive. Less welcome, perhaps, were the fleas, ticks and other biting insects which would have infested the furs on which people slept.

With the passage of time, the living spaces became more organised, and by the end of the ice ages there were separate areas for toolmaking, butchery, hide preparation, cooking and various other activities. The floors of tents and huts now had a covering of clay, rounded pebbles, or flat stone paving, and there are signs that these floors were swept clean quite regularly. Thousands of years later, when people had adopted a farming way of life, even workshops for toolmaking were removed from the living space.

Farming brought a new aroma into the household.

PREHISTORIC HARDBOARD

IN NORTHERN EUROPE, wattle hurdles were a common building material throughout prehistory, and even survived into the 19th century. They were made by weaving together slender twigs, usually from a hazel bush, to form a thin, strong, but slightly flexible sheet of building material. Wattle was the prehistoric equivalent of hardboard, but with holes that had to be filled to make it draughtproof. This was done by daubing mud or clay onto the finished structure; the combination is known as wattle and daub.

Animal dung might have been used as fuel if wood was scarce, and in certain parts of the world, during particular phases of prehistory, farming people shared their living quarters with domestic animals such as horses, cows or pigs. Often this was because the animals needed protection from raiders who stole stock during the night. In colder climates, the noise and disruption caused by having the animals indoors were no doubt offset by the warmth their bodies generated through the night.

ON THE MOVE

During the earliest phase of prehistory, before the invention of farming, wild animals and plants were the mainstay of all human groups, and most people kept on the move to be sure of finding food. As long as our human ancestors were nomadic, most of their shelters remained temporary affairs, quickly constructed from whatever was available, and soon abandoned. Where trees grew in abundance, leafy branches or dead wood could always be found easily, close to the spot chosen for the camp. Wood was undoubtedly the most common building material throughout the prehistoric world.

There were no nails to hold the wood in place,

EXTENDED FAMILIES

At certain times in prehistory, people chose to live in extended family groups under a single roof, and this required larger and more complicated buildings. Communal longhouses were typical of the farmers who lived in inland areas of northern and Central Europe during the late Stone Age, and also of Arikara Indians living in the Missouri river valley about 500 years ago.

with the result that judicious balancing and wedging were required to make a stable structure. With the invention of cord, made by twisting tough grass stems or other plant fibres together, the people of prehistory could lash one piece of wood to another – which became very important in creating more reliable and sturdy constructions. Animal sinews could have served the same purpose.

If trees were scarce, other plant materials might be employed for all or part of the shelter. In warm climates, building materials included palm leaves, woven plant matting, or long grass stems lashed into thick bundles and used to make 'grass huts'. Sheets of bark could be removed from certain trees, such as birches, without killing the tree, and this created a lightweight raw material that could be used for making shelters. It was even employed in places where wood was plentiful. The ancient Native Americans, or Amerindians, of the eastern woodlands of North America put birch bark to use, making boats and containers from it, as well as temporary homes in which birch bark formed the waterproof covering over a wooden frame.

HOMES MADE OF HIDE

As soon as prehistoric people had mastered the art of preserving animal hides, they acquired a versatile new building material that was flexible, strong, waterproof and windproof. The value of skins in creating a shelter was probably discovered independently by prehistoric people in many different regions. In Ice Age Europe, about 15 000 years ago, hides were used to make tents, supported by timber poles set together wigwam-style. The holes dug to take the tent poles have been unearthed at Pincevent in southern France, and the tents reconstructed by modern archaeologists.

HOME FIRES Cave-dwellers in northern climates needed fire to dispel the prevailing cold and damp.

The hides for these tents were probably taken along when people moved camp, because preparing hides was such a time-consuming business. Along with the hides, the tent poles may also have been carried, to conserve timber. Once people had domesticated pack animals, such as horses, the items that they carried around could be bulkier and heavier, and so the tents grew larger and more elaborate.

Nomadic herding people who have survived into modern times, such as the Khalkha Mongols, demonstrate just how large a tent can be. Their traditional dwelling, or *ger*, is a circular structure made of wood with a thick white felt covering. It is large, light and spacious inside, as much as 20 ft (6 m) in diameter with a high ceiling. The *ger* requires pack animals to transport it, but it can be erected in just 30 minutes by three people.

Where there was no wood at all, prehistoric people adapted other materials. Just as the hunters of the Central Russian Plain used the huge bones of mammoths, so people on the shores of Alaska employed long curved pieces of whalebone, erecting them in an arch, over which they laid skins. The time required to build with scarce and unpromising materials combined with an abundant food supply may have lead to a more settled way of life.

CREATIVE BUILDING

When living farther inland, away from the shore, prehistoric people in what is modern Alaska developed an ingenious method of building, using blocks of compacted snow, cut from snow drifts. We would know nothing of such houses, had not the descendants of such people – the Inuit or 'Eskimos' – survived into historical times, so that the building of snow-houses or igloos could be observed. It was a cunning procedure, in which one man stood within the growing structure, and stacked up the snow blocks in a spiral around himself. Another man stood outside, packing loose snow into the cracks between blocks; these quickly solidified into ice, making the igloo windproof. The blocks were carefully cut in advance to give them a slight slope from left to right, so that each rested its weight against the previous block in the spiral. A curve on both the outer and the inner surface meant that each new block leaned inwards slightly from the block immediately below.

When the overall structure was complete, the builders cut a door in the side and a hole for a window in the roof. With a show of real genius, they then made 'glass' for the window by enclosing the snow block they had cut away in a piece of seal-skin, allowing it to melt, and then packing it back into the window space until it froze again. When the sealskin was cut away, there was a block of clear transparent ice in the window.

Within the igloo, benches for sleeping and sitting on were built up from more snow blocks. It was warmer on these benches, away from the ground. Thick coverings of moss and fur prevented the body heat of the occupants from melting these pieces of icy furniture. A fire could be built in the centre of the igloo without causing the ceiling or walls to melt unduly, and the temperatures within might rise to 16°C (60°F). Only towards the end of the winter did the structure begin to melt. When parts of the roof began to fall in, the igloo was abandoned.

It would seem impossible for a house built of water to have left any trace in the archaeological

URBAN SPRAWL

The city of Tepe Yahya, now in Iran, had its beginnings over 7500 years ago, and was inhabited, with constant rebuilding, for about 5000 years. The mound left today is 60 ft (18 m) high and a third of a mile (0.5 km) in circumference. The village of Çatal Hüyük in Turkey, first inhabited 9000 years ago, and abandoned after about a thousand years, created a mound 50 ft (15 m) in height and covering 32 acres (13 ha).

record, yet there are signs of ancient igloos on the stark stony terrain of coastal Alaska. Very shallow circular depressions of greenish-grey are found, the colour created by lichens and mosses growing on the ground, benefiting from nitrogen and other mineral nutrients in the thin soil. These nutrients originally came from the fish and meat cut up there, within the igloo, over 3000 years ago. That this represents the remains of an igloo is something archaeologists could never have known had the building of igloos not survived into historical times. In the absence of this information, they would have interpreted the green circle as the sign of a tent. If ice is an unlikely building material, so too is mud, yet it proved its worth to prehistoric people of different continents. Wherever weather conditions are hot and arid for most of the year, mud houses are a possibility.

CITIES OF MUD

Mud can be daubed onto a structure built of wood or bone, or used alone. People make the very simplest mud buildings by slapping the wet sticky material into place with their hands, shaping and smoothing it, allowing the mud to dry a little, and then adding more to raise the wall higher. A more elaborate method is to form walls by

SNOW HOME   An Inuk igloo-builder today stands beside a small temporary igloo. In the past, far larger igloos were built, some of which housed several families.

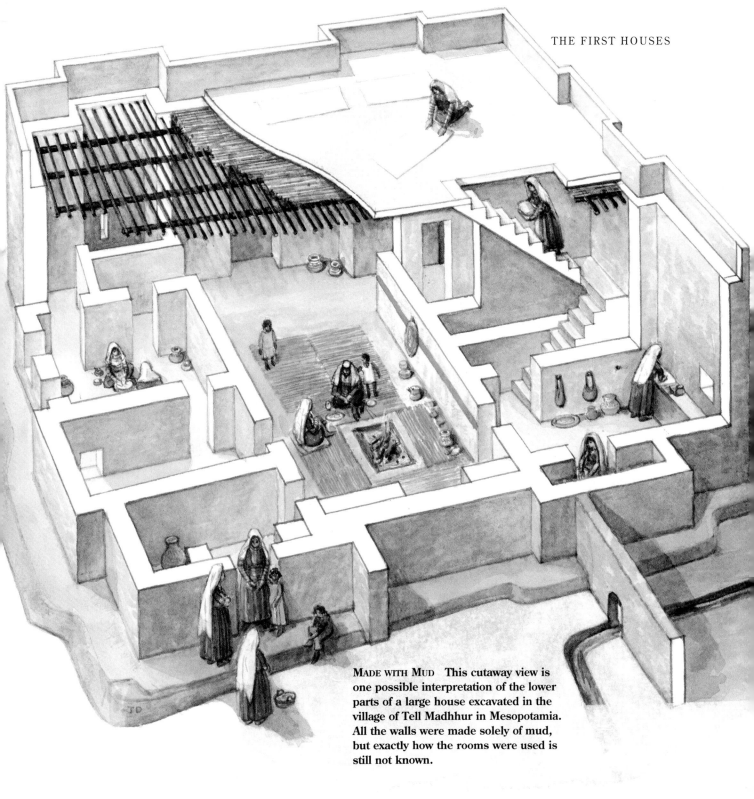

MADE WITH MUD This cutaway view is one possible interpretation of the lower parts of a large house excavated in the village of Tell Madhhur in Mesopotamia. All the walls were made solely of mud, but exactly how the rooms were used is still not known.

pouring the mud between wooden planks that hold it in shape until dry. Alternatively, the mud can be made into rectangular building blocks, mud-bricks, which are then used for building – a method known as adobe. The bricks are either shaped by hand or pressed into a wooden mould.

In a predominantly dry climate, mud buildings last remarkably well. The sun bakes the mud hard, with the result that it easily resists the impact of the seasonal showers. When rain does fall, it washes some of the mud down from the top of a mud wall towards its base, but far from weakening it, this actually helps to strengthen the building by reinforcing its base.

Mud buildings, their substance identical to the earth around them, merge into the landscape, both visually and literally. The effect of rain in thickening the lowest part of the walls, combined with the weight of the building pressing down, makes the wall bases ever more solid. In time, the compressed mud becomes rock hard and almost indestructible.

When a mud building finally burns down, or cracks and collapses with age, the base remains firmly in place. If another building is needed on the same site, the easiest course is to use the rubble of the upper parts of the building to fill in the cavities between the wall bases, so forming a level platform on which a new mud house can be built.

Rebuilding on the same spot was a common practice in prehistory, suggesting that people had strong affections for their particular place in the landscape. Where mud houses were rebuilt on the same site, the level rose steadily over the centuries, often to dramatic heights. Beginning about 8000 years ago, the prehistoric inhabitants of modern Turkey, Iran and neighbouring countries built

large towns of mud houses, constantly rebuilding on the same sites. The remains of these settlements still exist as huge tells, or artificial mounds, looming up from the surrounding plain.

On the other side of the world, and many millennia later, mud cities were built once again, in a completely independent burst of human innovation. Beginning about a thousand years ago, the Hopi, Hohokam and other groups of prehistoric Amerindians living in the hot dry lands of Arizona and New Mexico, used mud to build impressive pueblos. These consisted of many small accommodation units and storerooms, packed together to form a grand, imposing structure, several storeys high.

The Hopi used timber frames for their constructions, often importing the long beams from far away. Because these were so valuable, and might be re-used for another building at some future date, the imported roof timbers were not sawn down to the correct length – in a subsequent building a

longer piece might be needed. Consequently, the roof timbers often protruded from the sides of the buildings, giving Hopi architecture one of its most characteristic features.

BUILDING WITH STONE

Elsewhere in the American south-west, pueblos were built of stone, one of the most enduring building materials. Many pueblos have survived, but this is not always the case with stone buildings. Unfortunately for archaeologists, good building stone is such a precious resource that abandoned or tumbledown buildings were often demolished and the stone used for rebuilding, if not immediately, then in later centuries. This makes sites where stone buildings have survived particularly interesting.

Along the shores of the island of Orkney, in the north of Scotland, there are places where outcrops of the local stone, known as Old Red Sandstone, are worn down by the pounding of the Atlantic

waves into flat platforms of rock that extend from the shore into the sea. The rock, laid down as sediments under the sea 300 million years ago, has a layered structure, and when it splits it does so along neat horizontal planes.

Flat slabs of this rock can be obtained by inserting a sharply pointed piece of antler into a groove on the outer edge of a rock platform, and striking the antler with a hammerstone. With repeated strikes along the edge, a slab eventually breaks away. About 4500 years ago, many such slabs were being hewn out and carried inland, to a spot where a new village was being built.

The builders were some of the earliest farmers to live in the British Isles, still cultivating the land

DOGON VILLAGE In Mali, West Africa, where trees and building stone are both very scarce, the Dogon villagers stil! build all their houses from mud. It is a flexible material, and the buildings blend perfectly with the landscape.

entirely with stone tools. They had, by then, inhabited the site for 500 years, and their village needed rebuilding. The village which these farmers built – a model of orderliness and durability – has been preserved almost intact for modern inspection and is now known as Skara Brae.

What was remarkable was the degree of overall planning involved in this building programme at Skara Brae, the uniformity of the new houses, and the formality of their design. All of this suggests a group with enormous capacities for cooperation, self-discipline and forward thinking.

BUILDING SKARA BRAE

Not all the houses were built at once – there was a first phase of building, and then a second one some years later, perhaps when the next generation had grown up and needed more living space. Despite this time lag, the houses were built to an almost identical plan. Each house was roughly square inside and up to 21 ft (6 m) across, with the later houses being slightly larger. The stone walls were clearly meant to last or at least to keep out the severe winds of Orkney: they were up to 6 1/2 ft (2 m) thick. The regularity of the Old Red Sandstone blocks allowed the builders to make the walls very neat and regular inside, and to create a clean, squared-off shape to the house. Externally, however, the walls were highly irregular – a great jumble of projecting stones. This did not matter because the outsides were never seen again once the house was complete – all the houses were surrounded, up to the eaves, by a layer consisting of the rubbish of earlier generations. This rubbish was apparently collected from nearby rubbish heaps (known to archaeologists as middens) that had accumulated over the centuries. They contained fish

HOUSEHOLD GOODS
The inhabitants of Skara Brae left behind many possessions, including the bone beads of their necklaces.

and animal bones, shells of limpets, oysters and crabs, bits of eggshell, fragments of broken pottery (potsherds), blunted stone knives and axes, and the discarded flakes of flint from tool manufacture. The refuse of 500 years was spread over the whole site, entirely filling the space between one house and another. Enclosed, stone-lined passages snaked through the village, rather like tunnels, connecting the houses. This midden material helped to consolidate the houses and protect them from the cold.

The stone walls were probably roofed over with a pitched (sloping) roof made of timber, and then thatched with straw or heather, or covered with turf dug from the nearby ground. A third possibility is that thin slabs of stone were used to cover the timber beams of the roof. At one end of the village

BURIED VILLAGE The village of Skara Brae has now been excavated; when it was inhabited, however, the whole structure was roofed over with timber and possibly covered with thatch of straw or heather or with turf.

stood a workshop, where tools of stone were made.

On entering a Skara Brae house, the first thing that a visitor saw was a massive 'shelving unit' made of slabs of stone. This stood exactly opposite the entrance to each house, against the far wall, and its prominent position leaves little doubt that it was meant to impress.

STATUS SYMBOLS

What was kept on these shelves is a matter of debate. Perhaps hunting trophies – the antlered heads of deer, for example – were displayed. Or perhaps it was pottery, since certain pots were considered prestige items in prehistoric Europe, as in many parts of the world. The fact that the earliest flat-bottomed

pots in Britain were made at Skara Brae may be significant – the round-bottomed pots that preceded them were designed to rest in hollows on the ground, or on the coals of a fire, not on a stone shelf.

Some of the potsherds found at Skara Brae are elaborately decorated, while others are plain – perhaps the former sat on the shelf to be admired or to be used in some form of ritual, while the latter were used to hold water and cook the meals.

Meals were cooked over a large rectangular hearth at the centre of the house. The hearth was neatly edged with stones, and around this, in several of the houses, there were sturdy blocks of stone on which people could sit. Two large beds stood along the side walls, centrally placed in line with

SHOWING OFF Shelves, made from stone slabs, greet the visitor to a house in the village of Skara Brae.

the hearth. The beds were deep, stone-walled troughs, probably filled with springy heather and topped with soft furs for comfort. There are signs even of timber corner posts to each bed, which probably carried a canopy of furs above the sleepers for additional warmth.

The structure of the beds changed during the course of this last phase of building at Skara Brae. In the first houses to be built, the beds were set into alcoves in the side walls, with three sides of the bed consisting of the outer wall, and one of vertical stone slabs. Later on, when larger houses were built, there were no sleeping alcoves: vertical slabs formed three sides of the bed, the outside wall just one. In winter this arrangement was probably warmer, because the walls of the house would have felt cold and slightly damp. This is further evidence

of the way in which prehistoric people learned from their mistakes and constantly innovated.

Where a house has just two beds, scholars surmise that the children slept together in one of them, and speculate that the number of children per family was therefore not that high. In one of the later houses, there is a third bed built along one side wall, implying that families had grown larger.

CUPBOARDS AND LIMPET TANKS

Alcoves in the walls acted as cupboards at Skara Brae, but there were also curious little stone-walled tanks set into the floor, usually three in each house. These are daubed with clay, making them watertight, yet they are too small to be useful for holding drinking water or cooking meat – and, in any case, they are not next to the hearth as would

FORTIFIED HOUSES

IN TIMES OF TROUBLE, prehistoric people were forced to turn their houses into fortresses. Some of them responded to conflict by making secure houses below the ground, while others raised massive walls to keep out the enemy. The most impressive of these defended houses are the brochs of Scotland – individual dwellings built 2000 years ago, with walls up to 20 ft (6 m) thick and rising to over 43 ft (13 m) in height.

The broch was, in effect, a rather cramped cottage with walls thick enough for a castle. To achieve the extraordinary bulk of the walls, it was necessary to taper them inwards as the tower rose (otherwise there was a danger that the many tons of stone would simply collapse under their own weight). To guard further against collapse, there was a hollow built into the walls (rather like a cavity wall), which reduced their weight without reducing their thickness. Within this gap it was possible to build a small stone staircase which led up to rooms and a lookout post near the top of the broch.

There was just one entrance – a narrow passageway through the thick wall, which could be blocked off with a slab of stone or timber. As if this were not defence enough, the brochs often had a rampart and a ditch around them as well.

Within the broch, there was a stone hearth and some stone-built furniture. Partway up the tower were one or more timber-made galleries which ran around the walls, and it was here that people slept. Some scholars claim that they had a wooden roof over their heads, which may have sat on the stone towers of the brochs like conical hats.

If so, the brochs must have been a strange sight, like giant toadstools brooding over the landscape. Other authorities believe that the brochs were not roofed, but that the people relied on the sheer height of the walls to keep out the rain, which tends to fall diagonally rather than vertically in this windy part of the world.

Brochs were only built for a fairly short period, from about 100 BC to about 100 AD. Later settlements were often built in or around them, and the inhabitants seemed to have drawn comfort from their massive predecessors, as well as robbing the earlier structures for building stone.

On the Mediterranean island of Sardinia, similar stone towers were built over 3000 years ago. These towers, known as *nuraghe*, were undoubtedly for defence, but whether they were also inhabited on an everyday basis, as the brochs were, is open to question.

HOME AND CASTLE The brochs of Scotland – in this case, Shetland – had truly massive walls, surrounding a dark, cramped living space.

be expected of cooking troughs. Local people on Orkney were able to solve this puzzle. Within living memory, shellfish known as limpets had been used as bait when fishing, but they needed soaking in fresh water for several weeks to make them soft enough for use. The small tanks at Skara Brae could have been soaking tanks for limpets, one containing recently collected limpets, and others containing those collected earlier and almost ready for the fisherman's hook.

There may even have been indoor lavatories in these houses. Some small cells built into the house walls have drains leading away from them. These stone drains, lined with tree bark, all connect up with a main drain running through the village.

The remains of stone houses are found in many other parts of Scotland, though few have the formidable sense of order and symmetry that permeates Skara Brae. Some are oval or round in shape, others rectangular; and though many were built long after Skara Brae, they often display a haphazardness and irregularity. The overall impression is that there may be no linear progress in human affairs, no steady advance with the passage of time. Skara Brae suggests that local developments can be far in advance of, or far behind, or simply out of step with, the larger world beyond.

A religious factor could explain the fact that the houses are mostly oriented along a fixed compass direction, with the doorway-hearth-shelving axis running from north-west to south-east. This is the same orientation used for the chambered stone tombs built by people of this time, such as Maes Howe on Orkney. There is often a striking resemblance between the houses built for the living and the tombs built for the dead, not just at Skara Brae but elsewhere in prehistoric Scotland; and this all suggests a strong ritual or symbolic element in the design of dwellings. Perhaps the authority that sustained social order at Skara Brae was the authority of the dead ancestors, worshipped in the impressive tombs constructed nearby.

DOING WITHOUT WOOD

At a more practical level, the stone houses of Scotland allow archaeologists to trace, with unusual clarity, the process of learning to build without wood. As the forests of Scotland retreated in the

face of the stone axe, prehistoric people turned more and more to stone as a building material.

First, the walls were built of stone, with timber used for the roof, any internal partitions, and the furniture. As the centuries passed, and supplies of timber became increasingly scarce, stone was used in furnishing the houses, as at Skara Brae. Elsewhere, in houses that had once had internal timber partitions, these began to be made of stone, either very large slabs set vertically in the ground, or wall-like partitions constructed from small pieces of stone, as in the wheelhouses of Jarlshof in the Shetland Isles. These houses, built about 2000 years ago, are circular in shape with stone-built piers radiating like the spokes of a wheel.

The ultimate step was to make a roof entirely of stone, a feat requiring considerable skill. The stones of each wall have to be carefully stacked so that they bring the distant walls together in an arch, while still remaining fully supported and stable – a process known as corbelling. At Jarlshof, the first steps in this process can be seen: the walls curve in a little way above the stone partitions, but they

Reconstructing a Stone Age House

ARCHAEOLOGISTS have on many occasions tried to reconstruct prehistoric houses. One of these reconstructions took place at Aleslev in Denmark, where a longhouse originally built by early farmers was re-created. The house was about 49 ft (15 m) long by 20 ft (6 m) wide, yet it took 72 slender tree trunks to make the upright poles and rafters, 2000 stems of hazel and willow to make the woven wattle walls, 220 bundles of reed and rushes for the roof, and 9 tons of clay, straw and water, kneaded together with bare hands and feet, to make the sticky daub that waterproofed the walls. The whole business of collecting materials and building the house was

LONGHOUSE **Archaeologists have re-created an Amerindian house at Pamunkey, Virginia.**

estimated to have required 15 people working full time for ten days.

Archaeologists in Britain, working at a site near Peterborough, have reconstructed a Bronze Age roundhouse built with ashwood

and willow stems, daubed with clay, and roofed with thatch covered by turf. In America, too, archaeologists have reconstructed a Native American, or Amerindian, house at Pamunkey in Virginia, living and eating as Amerindians of about 1000 years ago. Rain waterlogged the thatch and the roof then collapsed, forcing the archaeologists to retreat to modern accommodation. Clearly, there was some construction technique known to prehistoric people that had not yet been mastered by their modern imitators.

stop short of a full stone roof, and the central hole must have been covered over with timbers.

The full corbelled stone roof was achieved in prehistoric Scotland, as evidenced by tombs such as Maes Howe. Whether this spectacular advance in roofing techniques was ever applied to everyday housing is debatable – there is no direct evidence

BELOW GROUND
This roundhouse from the Orkneys has a cellar that may have been used for storing food, or as a refuge from enemies.

that it was, although the uppermost stones of any roof would, in any case, have been the ones most vulnerable to dislocation by the weather or to removal by people making new buildings elsewhere.

DOWN INTO THE GROUND

For prehistoric people, whose houses generally lacked windows and had little natural light or ventilation, being below ground made little difference. Digging out a house was often a sensible alternative to building high walls up from the ground, and required no materials for the sides of the dwelling.

Subterranean living was not uncommon in prehistoric times. For example, it was practised by people in the Arctic, where it reduced the need for scarce building materials. Even where permanently frozen ground might prevent dwellings from being

THE LAKE-DWELLER OF NEUCHATEL

THE LAKE WATERS had fallen again, and it seemed like a good day to go back to the house and rescue the belongings they had abandoned when they escaped the recent flood. The man dragged his dugout canoe down to the shore and got it afloat.

It was the heavy rainfall of past weeks that had made the waters of Lake Neuchatel – now in Switzerland – rise, until finally they lapped at the door and began to flood the floor. The priority then was to get the children out quickly; everything else had been left behind. As he paddled the boat towards the house, a wind suddenly began to blow, churning the lake surface into waves. He wondered if he should turn back, but decided to keep going. It was the wrong decision.

As he reached the house, a strong wave rocked the canoe and pushed one end of it under the floor of the house. Normally, a boat would fit easily between the water surface and the floor, but because the water level had risen space was reduced. The canoe was now stuck beneath the wooden floor of the house, held tight there by its own buoyancy. The man tried to free it, but without success.

Towards the end of the day, a neighbour, seeing what had happened, came to the rescue in his own canoe. They tried again to release the trapped vessel, but had to abandon the attempt. As night fell, they returned to the shore in the second canoe, taking tools, bowls and other items from the house, but leaving the trapped boat behind. Over the ensuing millennia, it was gradually buried by lake sediments and eventually excavated by archaeologists in the 20th century. The site is now known as Auvernier-Nord.

LOG JAM Floodwaters probably trapped the canoe beneath the house.

completely underground, they could still be semi-subterranean, with at least 20 in (51 cm) below ground level. Settlements of the Punuk culture, about 1000 years ago, demonstrate these people's pragmatism in using what little they had, for the houses were partially buried, with the upper walls built of driftwood or whale jawbones, and the roofs made of turfs supported by whalebone rafters.

The earth irons out extremes of temperature. Even today, people living in the Martmata mountains of Tunisia, known as Troglodyte Arabs, dig out rectangular sunken courtyards, over 20 ft (6 m) deep, and excavate their homes from the earth around them. The houses are cool within, and the inhabitants gain welcome shade in the courtyard during the heat of the day.

In northern France and south-west Britain, earth houses – known as *souterrains* and probably used for storage or keeping animals – were common in prehistoric times, and they are found in Ireland and Scotland too. Some tribes of Amerindians living along the Missouri river about 1000 years ago built huge pit-houses, sunk about 5 ft (1.5 m) into the ground. These could measure up to 65 ft (20 m) in length and seem to have consisted of one large room with a central hearth and a hole in the roof.

LIVING ON THE LAKE

Houses built over water are surprisingly common in prehistory, despite their considerable technical difficulties. In the Swiss Alps during the late Neolithic and Bronze Age, people built their houses

LIFE ON THE LAKE   A crannog in Ireland, at Craggaunowen, has been reconstructed using Stone Age methods.

over the lake water, or on marshy ground along the shore, driving long wooden stakes deep into the sediments to hold their dwellings clear of the water below. In some cases, they also made a horizontal grid of timbers which was laid on the lake bed to stabilise the vertical piles.

These lake dwellings remained the buildings of choice for almost 2000 years, from about 4750 years ago to about 2750 years ago. No doubt there were advantages in living close to the lake water, which supplemented their crops with protein-rich fish. In some cases, they built on the shore as well, or on small islands on the lake, and it is not entirely clear why these people sometimes went to the trouble of building over the water itself.

THE CRANNOGS OF SCOTLAND

Stone Age people living in the highlands of Scotland over 5000 years ago built artificial islands on some of the lakes, known in Scotland as lochs. At Loch Olabhat on North Uist, the crannog was made by first building a wooden causeway out from the shore, and then dropping stones from the end of the causeway into the lake, until these formed an island of one or two houses which projected above the water; these were built of timber filled with wattle hurdles. The early houses on the crannog were later demolished and replaced by more substantial dwellings, with walls made of stone and earth.

Bronze Age farmers continued the tradition of building crannogs, though they often used brushwood and logs in building up the island, as well as stone. Some of their crannogs were not connected to the mainland by a causeway but had small harbours where boats could dock.

The jewellery and precious goods found on the crannogs suggest that the people who lived here were quite rich, and some scholars think that they may have been chieftains who commanded labour and food revenues from the people around. This would explain the need to make their houses secure by locating them on the loch, where they could defend themselves against rival chieftains.

There may be many more crannogs lying below the water levels of Scottish lochs which have yet to be identified. Indeed, one systematic survey of Loch Awe in Argyll showed the existence of 20 crannogs, mostly invisible beneath the water level.

A PREHISTORIC VILLAGE IN CHINA

THIS ARTIST'S RECONSTRUCTION of an early farming village from the Yangshao area of China is based partly on excavations, and partly on informed guesswork. The village dates from about 6000 years ago, and has one rather large building in the centre which was probably a communal area. It was about 36 ft (11 m) long and 33 ft (10 m) wide, with massive timber pillars based on sturdy stone supports.

The long entrance 'tunnel' may have served to keep out cold winds. The roof, which extended to the ground, was made of wooden beams and rafters, wattle and daub and thatched with straw. Although pigs were kept, the farmers also relied on game and fish for food.

SICKNESS AND HEALTH

Disease, injury and deformity were as much part of the human condition

in prehistoric times as they are today; some of them may have originated at

the moment when our distant ancestors first stood upright and walked.

GRAUBALLE MAN, one of the bodies found preserved in Danish peat bogs, lived about 2000 years ago in an Iron Age farming community. His teeth showed some dental decay, a few holes, and signs of inflammation in some of the roots. He was 30 years old when he died, and there is no doubt that he had suffered terrible toothache at times in his life. One tooth was missing, and must have been lost long before death because the socket was completely closed over.

Even though dental decay was uncommon, the teeth of our ancestors still suffered badly from their diet. As soon as early hominids began to dig roots and tubers from the ground, they inevitably ate grit along with their food. The grit leaves scratches on the tooth enamel which can be seen under a microscope. Once people began washing roots before they ate them, the scratches were fewer, but they reappeared when people started to use a stone grinding device known as a quern to make flour from seeds – firstly the seeds of wild grasses, and later those of cultivated cereals. They pushed another stone back and forth over the seeds on the quern to produce flour, and although they chose a robust type of rock to make the quern and grinding

TEETH AS TOOLS
A bow drill required downward pressure using a pad gripped by the teeth. Like many prehistoric activities, this wore the teeth down.

stone, it did generate microscopic grit which scarred the teeth and eventually wore them down.

This was just one of the ways in which teeth could be damaged. Coarsely prepared foods could be abrasive, such as the roots of the bracken fern, which the Maoris and the Aborigines gathered from the wild. Dried meat, or pemmican, requires a lot of chewing, and if eaten habitually it can wear down the teeth, as it did among some tribes of Plains Indians in North America.

Prehistoric people often used their teeth almost like tools – as a pair of built-in pliers, or a grinding machine, or a third pair of hands. There were drills for boring holes in bone and shell which required the driller to hold a mouthpiece of bone or wood between the teeth. Ancestors of today's Inuit or Eskimo chewed hides to soften them, and this took its toll of teeth and gums. Resin from birch trees was chewed by early European farmers to warm it up and make it workable, and then used to secure arrowheads to their shafts.

LIFESTYLE CHANGES

Many of these effects on the teeth were a result of people changing their diet, of moving to new areas, or of living in new ways to which their bodies were not yet fully adapted. Other human diseases were also caused by such changes. For example, prehistoric people living on the coast of Peru at a site called Paloma showed benign outgrowths on the small bones of the inner ear. Only the men suffered these growths, which were probably caused by regular diving for shellfish in very cold water.

If the human body was not fully adapted to diving in cold water, neither was it suited to living in chilly northern climates with short winter days. Sunlight falling on the skin is necessary for the body to make vitamin D, which helps bones to grow. When people moved north and began covering much of their skin

ANCIENT CURSE These crutches were made by prehistoric Anasazi people from the American south-west. Native Americans of many tribes had – and still have – a genetic predisposition to arthritic diseases.

can also be obtained from animal livers and oily fish, and this no doubt protected the hunters of Ice Age Europe. However, with the introduction of agriculture, such foods were consumed less often, and among early communities in Norway and Denmark skeletons show clear signs of rickets.

Such complaints are local in occurrence, but there was one universal scourge: osteoarthritis, a steady degeneration of the cartilage which provides a smooth surface within the joints. Osteoarthritis is largely caused by excessive use of the joints, and persisted all over the world throughout prehistory. Tombs on the Scottish island of Orkney, holding the remains of hundreds of early farmers, show that almost half the adult population was afflicted by osteoarthritis and other forms of degenerative disease of the bones or joints. The spine was affected more often than any other part of the body, which may be due to the heavy loads

with clothing, there was a risk of vitamin D deficiency, which leads to rickets. An obvious symptom of this is a bowing out of the leg bones, producing a bandy-legged appearance. Vitamin D

of stone and other building materials carried by these people. Especially striking is the occurrence of spinal osteoarthritis in children, suggesting that they did a lot of heavy work too.

It is not simply hard labour that over stresses the human skeleton. Even the act of walking upright on two legs is only 5 million years old, and the human skeleton has yet to adapt itself perfectly to this form of locomotion. The joints most often affected by osteoarthritis are those whose action has been most affected by this change in posture: hips, knees and the joints of the spinal column.

Chest infections and coughs caused by dust or smoke are also exacerbated by standing upright. Airways are equipped with mucus to envelop foreign bodies, and with frenetically beating hairs which drive the mucus out. An animal walking on

VITAL STATISTICS

Prehistoric people tended to be shorter than we are today, the average height for early farmers in Scotland being about 5 ft 7 in (170 cm) for men and 5 ft 3 in (160 cm) for women. The tallest men were no more than 5 ft 10 in (178 cm), while the tallest of the women was no more than 5 ft 4 in (163 cm). They made up for their lack of height in their powerful muscles, which testify to a life of hard physical labour.

NATURE'S MUMMIES ESCAPE DECAY

IN MOST PEOPLE'S MINDS, mummies are associated exclusively with ancient Egyptians. In fact, nature has ways of producing mummified bodies, in which the flesh, skin, hair and internal organs are perfectly preserved. These remains contribute greatly to our knowledge of the health problems of prehistoric people. Mummies can be produced by immersion in acidic bog water (which prevents decomposition by bacteria), by becoming entombed in ice, or by extremely dry sheltered conditions such as desert caves. Occasionally, bodies buried in oak coffins also become mummified, because the tannin from the wood prevents decomposition. Some prehistoric people practised deliberate mummification, including nomadic people known as Scythians who lived in Siberia 2400 years ago.

all fours has the hairs moving the mucus horizontally, but in an upright animal, such as a hominid, the hairs have to work against the force of gravity. This handicap to our natural defences undoubtedly made our ancestors – and ourselves – more susceptible to lung diseases.

Many prehistoric mothers and their babies must have died during childbirth. Occasionally, evidence of this is found, but often it has been lost because the fragile bones of a foetus or newborn child disintegrate. Clay figurines from Mexico, dating to Aztec times, show various abnormal deliveries that can be encountered during childbirth. These figures may have been used to teach midwives how to cope with such problems.

As prehistoric people began to experiment with farming, new threats to their health emerged. For example, the bones from Paloma in Peru show distinctive lines when X-rayed. These lines – a sign of arrested growth – seem to mark an annual season of food shortage among people who lived at a time when agriculture was just beginning. Once farming techniques were established, however, and the food supply was assured throughout the year, these lines are no longer found in the skeletons. People grew taller than ever before, and

their life expectancy increased, as they became better at growing crops and storing them for hard times.

Tilling of the land must have exposed people to soil-borne infections such as tetanus, which can prove fatal. It leaves no sign in the skeleton but other infections do, including tuberculosis. This debilitating infection is first seen about 4500 years ago among Stone Age farmers in Germany and Denmark. Although tuberculosis can be contracted by eating the meat of infected animals, the risk of infection grew when people began living in close company with domesticated cattle. Once the bacterium had infected the human population, it evolved into a type that was most closely suited to human physiology, and became a disease in its own right, distinct from bovine tuberculosis. Smallpox may have evolved from cowpox in much the same way; and measles from a virus which affected domesticated dogs.

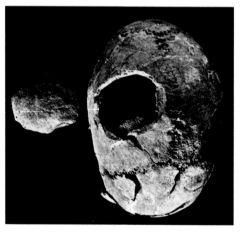

HOLE IN THE HEAD It seems as if plenty of prehistoric people needed a hole in the head – or thought they did. This trepanned skull, and the segment removed, comes from Dorset in England.

TOGETHERNESS AND DISEASE
The simple feat of living crowded together in larger groups increased the risk of infestation by parasites. Mummies of Amerindians from a site in North America show that 44 per cent of people were infested with head-lice; and Peruvian desert mummies tell a similar story.

HEALING HERBS   A Mentawai medicine man, from Siberut Island in Indonesia, prepares a herbal treatment.

Another study from North America, looking at skeletons from a site which was inhabited for thousands of years, showed that signs of bone infection increased as the population density rose: no doubt other infections followed the same pattern. One of the infectious viruses that leaves marks on the skeleton, the polio virus, was almost certainly present in human populations from very early times.

Migration into new areas often precipitates epidemics, either among the migrants or among the indigenous people they encounter. In the Arctic region, the invasion of Thule people led to a sudden decline in the indigenous Dorset people about 1000 years ago. It seems likely that the Thule people brought new diseases with them from their Asian homelands, and that these infected the Dorset people, hastening their decline.

PREHISTORIC MEDICINE

Few of the medical treatments practised by prehistoric people have left any trace for us today. One of the most striking exceptions is trepanation, the practice of cutting discs from the skull without breaking the delicate membrane below or damaging the brain; it was possibly used to treat severe headaches, mental illness, or even to let out evil spirits from the sufferers.

The earliest practitioners of trepanation lived in the Stone Age and used sharp stone blades. Some people died during the operation but others survived, as shown by the way the cut edges of the bone healed. Some people were operated on more than once – seven times in the case of one individual.

Other forms of common treatment may have included tattooing, applied to painful joints. Signs of tattooing are seen on mummified corpses, such as that of the man who fell into the Austrian glacier 5300 years ago. He had five groups of lines tattooed on his lower back, on either side of the spine. On the inside of his right knee, there was a mark in the form of a cross. On his left calf were three groups of lines, with more lines on the right foot and right ankle. Another cross-shaped mark appeared on the left ankle. It is possible that these tattoos, made by cutting the skin and then rubbing

LIFE EXPECTANCY

Despite exercise and a plain diet, prehistoric people did not live long; most died by the age of 40 or 50. Life expectancy for women was less than for men, a reverse of the situation today. This was undoubtedly due to the hazards of childbirth.

THE MAN FROM BROKEN HILL

PAIN HAD PERSISTED for a long time now, deep inside his head, intense and throbbing. It seemed to be located around his left ear, but he could not be sure. He simply had to bear it and continue with hunting, making camp and moving on.

The man lived in East Africa near a place called Broken Hill, now part of Zambia. An early representative of modern man, but with a skull giving a strong brow, he is known to archaeologists as Rhodesia man.

Then came a day when the pain became almost unbearable and, as the sun rose high at noon, he had

PAINFUL PAST The skull from Broken Hill with its telltale hole.

finally to stop walking. He sat down, put his head in his hands and then, strangely, felt moisture against his left hand. Taking it away, he saw a

thick, yellowish and foul-smelling liquid on the palm of the hand. He felt the side of his head and found where it was coming from – a small hole just below his ear.

The infection had finally eaten through the bone and forced a hole to the exterior. For several hours, the yellow pus continued to ooze through the hole. As it did so, the pain finally began to ease. The man walked down to a river and washed his head and his hands in the cool, clear water, washing away the pus. That night he slept well, far better than he had done for a long time.

in charcoal, were intended to cure the Ice Man of pains in his knee and ankle joints, backache, and a sprained muscle in his left calf. Similar tattoos have been found on mummified bodies buried 2400 years ago in Siberia, at a site known as Pazyryk in the Altai Mountains. Again, the tattoos were concentrated on the small of the back and the ankles. These bodies also had decorative tattoos, showing mythical beasts, intertwined in complex patterns, but were of a completely different kind from the treatment tattoos.

A few medical treatments may actually have been helpful. Early hominids living in Africa probably had an instinctive knowledge of medicinal herbs, as chimpanzees do. Once they moved away from the forests, such knowledge would have become redundant, but they may have experimented with other herbs, and found some, such as peppermint leaves and willow bark, with healing properties.

Amputation of a diseased or irremediably damaged limb was sometimes practised. The earliest-known case occurred among a group of Neanderthal people, living at Shanidar Cave in Iraq about 40 000 years ago, when a man's arm was amputated. Some prehistoric people also seem to have made splints for the purpose of setting broken bones. This is fairly common amongst prehistoric Amerindians in North America, but unusual in other parts of the world. It is surprising that such a

simple and obvious treatment was not more widespread. Most broken bones seem to have been left to themselves and often produced a misshapen bone as they set.

Even if medical treatments were simple and far from effective, there is plenty of evidence that people showed compassion towards the sick. There are signs of people being kept alive despite major disabilities. A man with a withered arm, who must have been a considerable burden to his family, is known from a cave in Israel. People with hare lips and cleft palates were kept alive even though they must have needed special feeding as babies, being unable to suck effectively. Dwarfs were fed and cared for, as were children with a congenital dislocation of the hip, who would never have been able to walk very fast or very far.

At Dolni Vestonice in Central Europe about 26 000 years ago, there lived an individual who walked with a limp and whose body was strangely misshapen. The right leg was shorter than the left and the spine curved to one side, giving the man – or it may have been a woman – a grotesque appearance. Furthermore, the skull was asymmetrical, distorting the face. These deformities may have been due to polio infection, or simply birth defects. Whatever the explanation, he or she grew to adulthood and was buried in a communal grave, which may have signified acceptance by the community.

SHAPING THE HUMAN WORLD

To transform the materials supplied by nature –

to make new objects, and to shape and modify the surrounding world –

is a deep-seated human desire. It first expressed itself in the simplest of

wooden tools and the crudest chipped pebbles, made millions of years ago.

With time, the technical skills of prehistoric people increased,

and tools became ever more sophisticated.

TOOLS AND WEAPONS

The first people belonging to our own subspecies, *Homo sapiens sapiens*,

devised a range of new ways for making stone tools and weapons:

from flint axes to spearheads shaped like laurel leaves.

IT WAS VERY DARK, cold and damp. The boy knew that he must show no fear, but as he lay face down on the clammy chalk floor of the mine, he felt a sense of panic and wished that he could wriggle backwards out of the gallery, up the rough wooden ladders and out into the strong summer sunlight above. Somehow he swallowed his fear and began hacking at the chalk as his father had shown him. It was the first summer that he had been allowed to go with the grown men to the flint mines, and he knew that he must not disgrace himself.

Using the pickaxe made from a red-deer antler, he hacked at the chalk, bringing it away in small lumps that he piled up behind him. Other boys collected it and carried it out of the mine. When he had cleared a reasonable area of chalk, he was told by his father to begin work on the layer of flint below – a band of black glassy rock, which was the object of their efforts.

The pick was far less effective against the flint than against the chalk, but eventually a piece came away, and the boy handed it back to others who carried it up out of the mine. Nearby in the sunshine sat two flint workers, and they quickly turned the newly excavated piece of flint into the head of an axe, although they did not give it the fine finish and sharp edge it would need to be a useful tool. The roughed-out axe was piled up with others that had been made that day.

BACK TO THE VILLAGE

In the evening, all the axe rough-outs were carried back to the village where the miners lived and where they grew wheat and barley, and raised cattle. Here, the axes would be finished off with delicate chipping, using wooden or antler tools, then bound to wooden handles to make the finished product. Some axes were for the farmers' own use, but most of them were carried far afield, to be traded for other goods produced in distant parts of the country.

Axe-heads were regarded as special, precisely because they had been quarried from so deep under the ground. The deepest mine shafts went down to 39 ft (12 m), passing two bands of flint on the way, until they reached a third band, where the effects of rain and frost had not been felt by the flint. This unweathered flint made a harder, sharper axe.

So valued were the axes from these deep mines that the demand ran to thousands, possibly tens of thousands, every year. The quarries, located in eastern England at a site known as Grime's Graves, were worked for at least 300 years, beginning about 4000 years ago. Exactly how far and wide these flint axes were exchanged is not known, but many must have been used to fell the primeval forests of Britain and to clear land for agriculture.

Also found in mine shafts at Grime's Graves were tools made of bone and antler. The shoulder blades and long bones of domestic cattle were adapted for

MINE SHAFT In their search for perfection, the miners of Grime's Graves dug down to the third level of flint, which was slightly harder than the layers above.

use as shovels to remove chalk rubble from the mine. Antlers from red deer were adapted by cutting off some of the side branches or tines: to make a simple rake all but two of the tines were removed, whereas for a pickaxe all the tines but one were removed, leaving a single sharp point that could excavate the chalk and flint. Occasionally, the picks were adapted to make simple axes, by adding an ox bone – this was shaped so that it had a sharp cutting edge on the outside and an inner hollow which fitted over the tine of the pick.

There are over 350 mine shafts at Grime's Graves, and those excavated so far have contained between 100 and 150 antler picks in each shaft. The demand for antlers discarded by deer stags in spring must have been enormous.

SHAPING THE WORLD

The finds at Grime's Graves illustrate several aspects of the prehistoric mind. One of these is the way in which people habitually looked at the world with an inventive and exploitative eye, always asking 'what could be made of this?' Picking up the antler of a red deer – perhaps intending to shape it into a hammer or some other rudimentary tool as his parents and grandparents had always done – a prehistoric farmer must have hesitated, turning it in his hands, thinking of other possibilities, imagining it with this or that tine removed, and computing new options for this familiar piece of raw material.

WORK IN PROGRESS **Three stages in the manufacture of a tool typically made by the Neanderthals are shown; the finished tool is on the right.**

> ## FLINT MINE
> One of the oldest stone mines in the world was established in southern Australia 24 000 years ago. The quarry at Koonalda Cave lies more than 250 ft (76 m) below the surrounding plain, and could only be reached by a sloping tunnel. Inside the cave, the flint miners needed artificial light. The camp fires and charcoal that have been revealed by excavation suggest that these prehistoric people used burning brush torches to light their way along the dark passages.

Similarly, when butchering the carcass of a cow to obtain meat, a farmer must have looked at the broad, flat shoulder blade and considered what use it might be put to – then thought of the accumulated chalk rubble down the mine, which took so long to pick up by hand, piece by piece. In the Near East, the same creative attitude to the world fashioned the earliest sickles from the rib bones of wild animals, setting tiny sharpened blades of flint into the inner curve of the rib to make a cutting edge.

The same ingenuity, shown by the Thule people of Alaska, turned the shoulder blades of walruses into snow-shovels. African hunters of the Kalahari made arrow-tips from porcupine quills, while in prehistoric Scotland spinal discs from stranded whale carcasses were used as tiny bowls for mixing red ochre pigment.

The discovery that animal skin could be sealed at its openings and inflated to form a float was made in several parts of the world. Inflated skins were often used as a means of crossing rivers or lakes, as in the Himalayas, but in the Arctic they were used when hunting whales – the float was attached by a line to the harpoon to keep the whale at the surface so that more harpoons could be thrown into its body.

Over the millennia, the first simple, easily made, multipurpose tools became more and more carefully made, with greater attention to detail. While the earliest stone tools were made with a few quick flaking movements, which removed large chips from the core stone, later tools were shaped by rough flaking, followed by fine flaking, and then retouching around the cutting surface.

In some toolmaking traditions, the flakes

SHOWPIECE This 'laurel-leaf' spearhead of flint, from Ice Age Europe, was made purely for prestige purposes.

themselves were used as tools, rather than the core – an efficient use of the stone. The lightweight flake tools were less tiring to use than heavy chopping axes, and each of the flakes could be used until it was blunt and then discarded. On the whole, stone tools became smaller, culminating in the microliths, which were tiny blades, some no longer than a fingernail, set into bone or wooden handles.

Toolmakers clearly took pride in their craft. During the Solutrean period in Ice Age Europe, beautiful 'laurel-leaf' spearheads were made, some of which were clearly never used. Thousands of years later, a similar practice of prestige items developed around the axe, a most vital tool, since it

STONE ON STONE Using a hammerstone, a toolmaker roughs out the shape of a flint tool.

enabled Stone Age communities to clear away woodlands for agriculture. Beautifully polished axes made of a green stone known as jadeite may have been exchanged, given as gifts, or displayed as status symbols – but they were never actually used. One was placed as an offering in the marshy Somerset Levels, beside the timber walkway now known as the Sweet Track.

Grinding and polishing axes only became popular once farming was widely practised, and modern experiments in toolmaking show that it was enormously time-consuming. A flint axe can be roughed out by flaking in less than half an hour, but the process of grinding, which involves rubbing sand and water against the axe using a wooden implement, takes between three and nine hours.

Another interesting discovery to emerge from experimental toolmaking is that the techniques are far from easy to master, and that some individuals show a greater aptitude than others. Perhaps, in prehistoric times, there were expert toolmakers who supplied others in their group with equipment.

PERISHABLE PARTS

Anthropologists studying a group of present-day Amerindians, known as the Athapaskans, who live just south of the Arctic, looked at their hunting and fishing equipment with a view to predicting what would survive in the archaeological record. The hunting gear included a spear, a wooden bow, arrows, a quiver made of goat skin, a bone club, a

SOME of the most ingenious prehistoric implements were made by Arctic hunters, the ancestors of today's Inuit or 'Eskimo'. About 2000 years ago, the earliest of the Thule people, living around the Bering Sea, invented the toggling harpoon, a device for use in hunting heavy prey such as whales and walruses. When the tip of the harpoon strikes the sea mammal, it becomes embedded beneath the thick blubber, lying parallel to the skin surface in such a way that it cannot be dislodged if the animal tries to swim off at speed or rubs hard against an ice ledge. The tip (which detaches itself from the rest of the harpoon) is tied to a line, which allows the hunter to reel in the exhausted animal.

HUNTER'S WEAPON An Amerindian flint arrowhead, found on a ranch in Georgia: the wooden shaft would have been attached with glue and twine.

skinning knife, and a hunting bag. If abandoned and buried, all that would survive of this complex array of equipment, the anthropologists decided, would be the iron tip of the spear, one iron arrowhead and the decorative beads used on the bag – and perhaps a few of the items made of bone and antler. The fishing equipment consisted of a large forked fish spear, a fishing net with floats and other attachments, fish-hooks, lines and weights. All this equipment is made from wood, plant fibres or tree bark, with just a few fine bones making up the fish-hooks and the central prong of the fish spear. The anthropologists predicted that none of this well-crafted fishing gear would survive.

This study of the Amerindians emphasises the importance of perishable materials, such as wood, plant fibres, bark, tree resin, sinew and animal hide, in equipping prehistoric people for survival. Such materials would have been used extensively, yet they hardly ever survive, except in specialised conditions: for example, in a dry and sheltered spot, such as a desert cave; or if enclosed by ice; or if submerged in boggy areas where acidic water prevents bacterial decomposition. These are exactly the same conditions as those that mummify human bodies; which is why a few sites, such as the desert caves of Peru, or the peat bogs of northern Denmark, provide us with such rich evidence about everyday life, yielding up mummified bodies, clothing, wooden tools, cord and basketry. For example, from Danger Cave in Utah come pieces of twined matting, coiled basketry, rough cloth, rope and wooden handles, and arrow shafts; the baskets were evidently used for gathering berries, nuts and grass seeds.

Many delicate items that would normally have perished have been preserved by the ice of the Arctic, including a pickaxe with a wooden handle and a sharp piece of bone for the blade, the two lashed together with leather thongs. A bolas, used for hunting birds, was found at the same site – a house buried by blocks of sea ice, blown ashore during a wild storm 500 years ago. It had been made from

TOOLS OF CLAY

In prehistoric Mesopotamia, stone was in short supply, as were other raw materials from which to make cutting tools. The early farmers who lived here sometimes made sickles out of baked clay, since there was nothing else available.

CAUGHT! A long-legged bird becomes entangled in a bolas thrown by a prehistoric inhabitant of the Arctic.

strands of sinew, knotted together at one end and attached at the other to five small pieces of pierced bone. By skilful throwing of this device, Inuit hunters could entangle the legs of wading birds, bringing them down in flight. Also found here were leather hunting bags and a wooden bowl sewn together with three rows of leather-thong stitching.

The ice of an Austrian glacier, which engulfed a hunter 5300 years ago, preserved wooden arrow shafts, neatly twisted string made from plant fibres, pieces of sinew destined to bind arrowheads to their shafts, a quiver made of animal hide, and two containers made from

STONE MACEHEAD A pierced and rounded stone, wedged on a pole, made an efficient digging tool – to be used with an up-and-down movement. This finely carved example is from Scotland.

birch bark carefully folded and sewn together. A dagger with a sharp stone blade had a handle crafted from ashwood, and was carried in a scabbard of plaited fibres obtained from lime trees.

Waterlogged sites have yielded similar artefacts, greatly enlarging our understanding of the tools used in prehistory. From the Swiss lakes where, 4000 years ago, people lived in houses built on stilts over the water, comes an axe with a sharp blade of polished nephrite stone, carefully set into a socket carved from antler, then mounted in a handle of ashwood.

THE FIRST WEAPONS

While hunting implements such as clubs and spears could also have been used to fight and injure people during the earliest phases of prehistory, there is little sign of this in the human remains – no crushed skulls and no 'parry fractures' to the arm bones suffered when fending off a heavy blow.

Some of the earliest evidence of warfare comes from rock paintings in Australia. The oldest of these may date back as much as 10 000 years, and show individuals or small groups of people fighting with boomerangs and spears. With the passage of time, these pictures change to show larger battles, with more developed weapons such as three-pronged spears and spear-throwers. Several of the warriors are wearing special headdresses, which

FLINT MASTERPIECE This finely crafted Danish flint dagger was made about 3600 years ago, by which time such weapons were buried alongside their owners. Daggers indicate aggression towards other human beings – they are of little value in hunting.

add to the impression that warfare had become a regular occupation by this time. Archaeologists relate this to a change in climate at the end of the ice age, when sea levels rose all around the world, flooding land which had previously been vital for hunting and food gathering. This reduction in space may have led to competition and conflict.

There is less evidence for warfare in other parts of the world at this time, despite similar rises in sea level and changing pressures on human populations. Warfare only seems to have become widespread with the development of farming and more complex settled societies. It seems that the existence of stored food and other valuable items which could be looted by the victors encouraged violent conflict. Hitherto, there had been little to be gained by violence, and there had been plenty of food-rich land into which people could move if they wished to avoid sustained conflict with others.

SLINGS AND ARROWS

Once violence and warfare became part of human life, specialised weapons were developed. These included daggers for fighting at close quarters, the blades made initially of stone and then, later, of bronze and iron. Bows and arrows proved particularly useful in warfare, although they had originally been developed for hunting.

The bow and arrow were only invented at a fairly late stage in prehistory, after the end of the ice age.

GIVING TOOLS TO THE DEAD

AT a farming village on the River Bolan, in what is now Pakistan, a young man died about 8000 years ago. According to custom, relatives placed his body on its side before rigor mortis set in, rested his head on his hands, and flexed the knees, so that it looked as if the dead man was merely asleep.

Placing the body in the grave, they put pairs of carefully worked flint blades beside him, in a long row stretching from the crown of his head down the line of his back.

There were 16 blades in all, representing hours of craftsmanship. An axe of polished stone, also painstakingly made, was placed nearby, along with three flint cores from

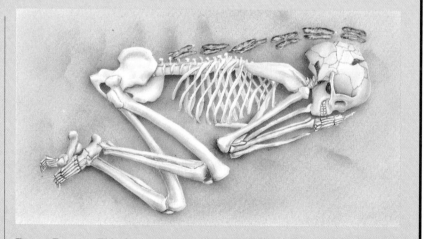

RITUAL BURIAL This farmer's grave from Pakistan contained flint tools.

which more blades could be struck. Finally, they placed nine tiny 'microlith' blades, turquoise beads and a basket waterproofed with tar. Only when equipped with these could the dead man be buried. What was necessary in life was also needed by the spirits of the dead.

KILLED BY AN ARROW

IT WAS CLEAR that the battle was lost. The man was trying to escape along one of the causeways out of the heavily defended enclosure, making a run for it with his child in his arms. He may have turned at the last moment, seeing that there were enemy archers ahead, but they had already taken aim and fired.

He died from a single stone-tipped arrow, which penetrated his back and went deep into the chest cavity. As he toppled forwards into the ditch below, the child began screaming, but the screams soon stopped. The weight of the man had stifled the child, lying crushed beneath his body in the ditch.

Above them, the wooden ramparts of the Stepleton enclosure, on Hambledon Hill in the west of England, blazed brightly. They had been set alight by the attackers who had overwhelmed the resistance and were now streaming into the enclosure. The flames leapt high into the sky until the charred timbers finally weakened and the whole structure collapsed into the ditch – both the timbers and the mass of chalk rubble which they contained. The bodies of the man and child were preserved beneath this mass, to be excavated 4600 years later.

BOWS AND ARROWS **This section from a rock painting in Zimbabwe shows hunters with bows and arrows; they are at least 5000 years old.**

This coincided with the disappearance of large mammals such as the woolly rhinoceros, mastodon and mammoth, which had been the staple diet of ice age people. These great giants could best be hunted at close quarters by groups of hunters, who bravely approached them and thrust stone-pointed spears through the thick hide of the animal. With the end of the ice age, there was a gradual change in the animal prey available, from large, lumbering creatures to the small and the fleet of foot, such as rabbits, deer and birds. Spear-throwing was rarely successful with such prey, and bows and arrows were used instead.

The stone and sling had similar attributes. Like the bow and arrow, it could be applied to both warfare and hunting. The sling, usually made of animal hide, did the work of the bow, with the stone flying in place of the arrow. Although it preceded the bow and arrow, the sling remained the preferred weapon of some prehistoric people for thousands of years. It had the great advantage of needing little crafting, unlike bows and arrows whose creation requires many hours of labour.

One good stone-tipped arrow, skilfully shot, can kill an opponent outright. An Amerindian skull was found at Buena Vista in California, with a stone-tipped wooden arrow shaft driven through the right eye. The arrow had been descending as it struck the man, and it penetrated his skull so forcefully that it emerged behind his left jaw.

Only with the discovery of metal smelting did prehistoric people invent swords. By then the 'arms race' was on: close on the heels of swords came defensive items such as shields, helmets and breastplates, then larger and sharper swords to cut through these defences.

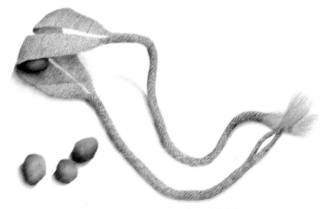

DEFENCE WEAPON **The sling was a formidable weapon in the hands of an expert. This one was found at Danebury in the south of England.**

POTTERY AND METALS

Using fire as a tool, prehistoric people turned soft wet mud into

hard rock-like pottery for containers and ritual vessels, and rock-like ores into

sharp shining metal for jewellery, farming implements and weapons.

THE EXPLOSION echoed through the village, and people ran from their houses to see what had caused the noise. At the far end of the village, a small fire smouldered in a pit in the ground and beside it stood the potter, surrounded by fragments of a pot. He explained that he had experimented with clay from a different riverbed, because his usual supply was almost exhausted. Something about the new clay, however, was different, and when the finished pots were fired they had exploded. He assured them that the problem could be solved – perhaps by adding some finely chopped straw to the clay, or some animal dung, or a little more sand than usual.

Firing can destroy pots, and does so regularly when people are working with a new source of clay. Not all explode – they may crack into pieces, or large flakes may come away from the surface. Sometimes pots survive the firing but disintegrate when they contact the air afterwards, because they are chemically unstable.

Clay is transformed into pottery by heat, but the metamorphosis is a dramatic one which can go disastrously wrong. Like metals, the starting material is quite different from the finished product, with fire the crucial intermediary. In this sense, pottery and metals are fundamentally different from most of the other raw materials used by prehistoric people, such as stone, wood, bone or plant fibres. Working with clay or metals therefore takes a certain willingness to take risks, even for an experienced potter or smelter. The initial process of

FEMALE FORM **One of the first clay artefacts, this baked clay figurine, from Dolni Vestonice in the Czech Republic, is more than 27 000 years old.**

invention, carried out by people in the remote past, required a truly remarkable leap of imagination, along with dogged persistence and an ability to experiment intelligently.

Prehistoric people had plenty of opportunity to observe the changes that fire could make to clay, and to examine the hard, stony substance that remained. They often spread clay over the floors of huts or tents, and sometimes used it to build up a hearth if large stones were not available. Clearing away the ashes the next day, they would have noticed that the clay had been transformed.

At first, this discovery was not put to any practical use. The first clay artefacts are small figurines modelled from clay at a site known as Dolni Vestonice in Moravia, Central Europe, where mammoth-hunters camped 27 000 years ago. Most of the figures are of the animals which they hunted for food or furs: the heads of bears, wolves and foxes, with the occasional mammoth, rhinoceros, horse, reindeer or bison also represented. Clay was modelled with a few deft movements, squeezing and pinching, and then tossed into the flames. Some of the pieces have not been modelled but simply pressed to produce a thumbprint before being fired. There are 2000 of these figurines and fingerprinted lumps in all. Only one figure is different – a more carefully crafted statuette of a plump woman, similar to the buxom 'Venus figurines' made from stone or ivory and found scattered across Ice Age Europe.

It was to be almost 15 000 years before the first manufacture of pottery vessels, and this development occurred, not in Central Europe, but in the Far East, probably in Japan.

Fragments of the oldest pots on Earth – some 12 700 years old – have been found at Fukui rock shelter, at the southernmost tip of Japan, near Nagasaki. These fragments are terracotta in colour, and fairly small, but they come from well-made pots that were delicately decorated with the impressions of twisted cord – clearly the work of an experienced and painstaking potter.

Ancient fragments of pottery, or potsherds, come from another Japanese site, Kamikuroiwa cave, while there are finds from Pengdoushan in China that are between 9000 and 10 000 years old. Ceramic skills advanced quickly in this part of the world, and some early pots are surprisingly elegant, such as the three-legged jugs made by Stone Age farmers in China around 6000 years ago. A separate tradition of painted pots, known as Yangshao, was equally ambitious and creative, as were the increasingly elaborate Jomon pots of Japan which developed from the early experiments at Fukui rock shelter.

In the Near East, pottery was first used about 8000 years ago, in early farming communities such as Jericho and Jarmo. This was probably an independent development, not influenced by any other part of the world. In the New World, pot-making was a

HIT AND MISS Firing in a pit, with the flames licking the pots, is a risky enterprise, and many pots break in the process.

completely independent invention, too, probably beginning in South America about 5000 years ago. It was here that the expressive capacities of pots were stretched to the full, especially among those that incorporate human figures, faces or animals.

FINDING CLAY

In most parts of the world, clay is found fairly easily: in riverbeds, or in the ground beneath the soil layer. It is then dried and pulverised, so that plant roots, lumps of wood and large stones or pieces of grit can be removed. The dry, powdery clay is then mixed with water to form a stiff, workable material.

Although some clays are naturally easy to work and fire well, this is not true of all; adding other materials can often improve the properties of a clay. Prehistoric people living on Motupore Island, a small island off New Guinea, excavated their clay from various points in the narrow strip of land between the steeply forested mountain slopes and the mangrove swamps and beaches of the coast.

They discovered that the clay could be worked more easily if sand was added, but there was a shock in store. Within a few weeks of firing, the pots began to crack and crumble until only a pile of tiny clay particles remained. We now know that the problem was caused by tiny fragments of shell in the sand, which decomposed when the firing temperature exceeded 760°C (1400°F) to produce an unstable compound, calcium oxide. When calcium oxide encounters water vapour in the air, it absorbs

TRIPOD POT Three-legged pots from the Far East, such as this jug from China, showed a sophisticated design that persisted for thousands of years; it is 5000 years old.

it rapidly in a violent chemical reaction, and it was this which was destroying the pots.

We will never know how these people discovered the solution to their problem, but we do know that they started to use sea water when moistening the powdered clay, rather than fresh water. The salt in sea water reacts chemically with the shell during firing, and calcium oxide is not produced.

CHAIN REACTION

This same technological advance occurred quite independently among prehistoric Amerindians living on the upper Mississippi valley, and was part of a 'chain reaction' in which one change in lifestyle led to a series of others. These early hunters and farmers made a transition to more intensive forms of agriculture about 1200 years ago, which involved moving into the fertile valleys around the major

COILING TECHNIQUE A large pot is built up by adding long 'snakes' of clay; each coil is then smoothed vigorously into the one below.

rivers. The clay here was different from that in their former homelands and proved very difficult to use. When their new pots began to disintegrate after firing, they too added salt. Their problem was that salt was in short supply in the area.

Farther south in the central Mississippi valley, however, there are many salt springs, from which the local Amerindians in the area obtained salts by evaporating spring water in long shallow basins. Spurred on by the need to make usable pots, the people of the upper Mississippi began trading with those of the central Mississippi to acquire salt. This led in turn to the exchange of other valuable items and to the development of special trading and cultural centres at sites known as Cahokia and Angel.

MAKING THE POT

For the greater part of prehistory, pots were made without the wheel, using a technique known as 'hand-building'. One simple method is to roll clay into a ball, push a thumb into the centre to make a hollow, and then gently to squeeze the clay between the thumb (which is on the inside) and the fingers (which are on the outside), rotating the pot all the time so that the pressure is spread evenly. The result is a small bowl which, with experience and care, can be made to curve inwards again, so that it is quite narrow at the neck. Making a large bowl by this method is difficult, because the size of the pot is limited to the size of the potter's hands.

A better method of making large pots, however, is coiling, whereby the potter begins with a flat or

AN EARLY DEATH

ABOUT 4000 YEARS AGO, a baby died in the west of England, at a site known as Normanton Down. Eleven bodies were buried there, most of them children, some singly, others in pairs. The burials were grouped together in a mound, known as a barrow, and surrounded by two ditches. It seems likely that the children were victims of an epidemic, perhaps diphtheria, which could strike suddenly and wipe out almost all the children in a settlement.

The baby, who was between two and six months old, was one of the last to die. Its body was placed across the entrance into the barrow, along with that of a nine-year-old. The older child had an ordinary, normal-sized beaker placed alongside, while the baby had a tiny beaker, which had clearly been made specially for the burial. This was not a vessel that had ever been used by the baby or anyone else in life, but a purely symbolic vessel. In Bronze Age Europe, the beaker was obviously far more than just a useful container.

FOOD AND FUNERAL RITES Pottery vessels had different uses. The decorated bowl on the left, used by early farmers in the east of England, was probably a container for food; the vessel on the right is a funerary urn, used for ashes of the dead, and was left in a barrow (burial mound) in the west of England.

inside the pot with one hand, while a flat wooden beater wielded in the other hand struck the pot on the outer surface. Some pots were left plain: simple utilitarian vessels to be made as quickly as possible. But many were decorated with enormous care and a great deal of artistic expression. Decoration sometimes formed an integral part of pot-making. When pots were thinned and enlarged with a beater and anvil, cord might well be bound around the beater to leave its distinctive impression on the pot. Cord was also used in more formal ways, to be pressed into a pot and so produce neat repetitive patterns. In Japan, during the Jomon period, string was wound around cylindrical sticks in clever knotted patterns, so that when the stick was rolled over the surface of the pot it produced an intricate design.

Cord-decorated pots were independently invented by prehistoric people in many other parts of the world, including northern Europe and North America. Some of the most complex patterns were made by creating a crochet-like net of plaited and knotted strings, which was placed over the finished pot and pressed in to produce the pattern.

Another method of decoration was to make cuts and marks on the

bowl-like base and then adds long worm-like pieces of wet clay, coiling them around onto the upper rim of the growing pot. The edges of both the pot and the new addition must be roughened and wetted to ensure that they stick, and there is also a smoothing process with the fingers, which blends the new coil into the clay below. A skilled potter can make large pots with coiling, some up to 3 ft (1 m) tall, which are useful for storing grain or other produce.

An entirely different approach is to roll out flat pieces of clay, as one might roll out pastry, and then use these to build up a pot, joining pieces together by roughening their edges, wetting them, and then smoothing over the join. This method, known as slabbing, was rarely used on its own in prehistoric times, but was sometimes combined with another technique such as coiling.

DECORATING THE POTS

Once the basic shape of a pot had been made, it was usually left to dry for a while, so that the clay became harder. At a certain stage, known as leather-hard, the clay is fairly strong and will not lose its shape, yet the surface is still soft enough to be cut, shaved down, scraped to make the walls thinner, or decorated. Walls could also be thinned by beating, a method which also increased the dimensions of the pot and made it slightly stronger. A large smooth pebble was used as an anvil, held

EARLY WHEEL
A simple wheel, kicked from time to time, rotates the pot for easier coiling and smoothing. It does not spin fast enough, however, to allow the potter to 'throw' pots – the modern technique.

pot using fingernails, large feathers, reeds, the corrugated edges of shells, special combs carved from wood or antler, or pieces of finely tipped bone. The idea of painting pottery, however, was far less common in prehistoric times. Glazing was also rare, but a pot could be made waterproof by applying a layer of pine or birch resin to the outside.

Styles of decoration, like methods of making pots, were a matter of tradition. From time to time, some creative individual would make a small variation to the age-old patterns, or even add some completely new element; and in this way, the styles gradually evolved, often developing into distinctive local variants.

THE MEANING OF POTS

It may well be that, for certain groups at certain times in prehistory, the true value of a pot lay not so much in its usefulness as in its form, its decoration, its ritual associations and its social value – either as a valuable item of trade or as a status symbol.

The existence of pots decorated with complex patterns, in which the decorative network of string was used once only and then discarded, suggests that each pot was intended to be unique. Burials, especially those of Bronze Age Europe, also point to the fact that people attached some special significance to pottery. Between about 5000 and 4000 years ago, pots known as beakers were regularly

GIANT POTS Farmers who grew grain and needed to store it required very large pots; making a pot of this size was a highly skilled process.

buried with individuals in their graves. These beakers are shaped like inverted bells and are decorated with neat and complex patterns of lines, which were made by pressing cord or combs into the clay.

It is widely agreed that the beakers were used as drinking vessels, possibly for an alcoholic liquid intended to fortify the spirit of the dead person for its journey out of this life. At one Bronze Age burial in Scotland, the presence of pollen from a lime tree all around the beaker laid a tantalising trail of

THE EXPERTISE OF THE POTTER

POTTERY is not simply dried and hardened by fire – it is also chemically changed, clay minerals becoming fused together in a process known as ceramicisation, or ceramic change, at a temperature of at least 550°C (1020°F). After a successful firing, water cannot soften the clay again, although many clays remain permeable to water because there are tiny channels penetrating the hardened pottery fabric that allow water to percolate.

This is not always a disadvantage. In a hot climate, permeable vessels can be used to store water and keep it cool through constant evaporation from the surface of the pot. Adding materials such as straw, grass or animal dung to the clay will make a more porous pot, since these materials burn off during firing to leave open spaces within the pottery fabric.

In some parts of the prehistoric world, potters seem to have

mastered their craft well enough to make specialised water pots with a particular type of clay that suited their purpose. But in the early days of potting, they had to make a pot that could be fired without breaking. Straw and other perishable materials help a pot to survive firing by opening up channels that allow steam to escape from the clay in the early stages of firing: it is the build-up of steam that causes pots to explode.

PAINTED PLATE **This pottery plate from the city-state of Ur in Mesopotamia has a bold painted design.**

clues. The nectar of lime trees is collected by bees, and lime pollen can easily find its way into honey. This has led historians to suggest that honey was probably fermented by people around this time to form an alcoholic drink known as mead, which was in the pottery beaker when its owner was interred in the Scottish soil. The problem with this theory, however, is that lime trees did not grow in Scotland 4000 years ago, but they did grow in the southern part of Britain. There must have been trade then,

either in the mead itself, or in the honey from which it was made.

In many other parts of the world, elaborately decorated pots were made largely for ceremonial use. About 1000 years ago, groups of Amerindians living in New Mexico, along the river Mimbres, made exquisite ceremonial bowls, painted with stylised human figures and geometric designs. These masterpieces of artistic expression may have been used in the house, but their ultimate

FINDING ALTERNATIVES TO POTTERY

LONG before pottery became available, there were containers of many other materials. Skins could be made to hold water; gourds or ostrich eggs made good drinking vessels; and baskets could be tightly woven and daubed with clay or resin to make them waterproof. To hunter-gatherers, these lightweight containers were far more valuable than pottery, which was cumbersome and fragile.

Even among settled people, pots were sometimes replaced by containers of other materials, such

POTTERY SUBSTITUTE Tree bark was a readily available material from which to make receptacles; this makeshift dish contains hazelnuts.

as bowls and platters carved from stone. In prehistoric East Africa, stone bowls were widely used, and in southern Britain, at Kimmeridge Bay, the soft black rock known as shale was cut to make bowls. For Amerindians of the eastern woodlands of North America, making a container from bark was a quick and simple procedure.

---

destiny was to be buried, usually placed upside down over the head of the dead person. Before the burial, a small hole was chipped in the base of the plate, a way of ceremonially 'killing' its spirit.

Pottery was also used to make portrait vases in South America about 2300 years ago, in the southern Mississippi region about 900 years ago, and in Mesopotamia about 6000 years ago.

THE FIRST METALS

No one could have thought that those tiny beads, with their unusual lustrous sheen and orangey colour, were the first sign of a technological revolution that would change the course of human life. The beads were made at Cayönü-Tepesi in Turkey about 9000 years ago, from pure copper metal, which is found in the earth in a few parts of the world and is known as native copper.

The people of Cayönü-Tapesi had collected their copper about 12 miles (20 km) north, at a site now known as Ergani Maden. However, the amount of copper they found was very small, which restricted its use for at least 2000 years. This did not prevent the people of Cayönü-Tapesi from experimenting with the new and exotic material, and they discovered that it could be hammered into different shapes. They found that it became hard and then

brittle if hammered for too long, and that heating it gently in the fire until it glowed red softened the brittleness. This process, known as annealing, eventually became commonplace among metalsmiths, although these early metalworkers did not fully master the technique.

Native copper was also available in Baluchistan on the Indian subcontinent 8000 years ago, where copper beads were made, and in the Balkans, where it was first used 7500 years ago. From here, metalworking spread southwards into Greece. The items made were usually decorative pieces such as beads, or simple utilitarian articles such as pins, for which copper was more suitable than stone or bone.

Throughout this era, copper was a prestige item – a rare, curious, exciting material, on a par with amber or lapis lazuli. The giant step in metal use, however, was to obtain copper from rocks, known as ores, that contained it in its mineralised form. The problem for these prehistoric innovators was one of recognising that the ores contained metals, since there is nothing coppery about the appearance of malachite and azurite, which were the first compounds to be smelted. They were beautiful in their own right, however, the malchites a lustrous greeny-blue like the wing feathers of a kingfisher, and the azurite an iridescent sky blue.

CREATING COPPER **These hearthstones were found in southern Israel, where copper ore was smelted about 4000 years ago.**

The transformation of malachite or azurite into metallic copper requires temperatures of about 1100°C (2000°F). Exactly how this important discovery was made is not known, but it occurred at least twice: once in Eurasia, probably in the Balkans, over 6000 years ago; and once in the New World, in South or Central America, about 2000 years ago. Some experts think that smelting may also have been discovered independently in the Far East over 4750 years ago.

MINING FOR METALS

With the invention of smelting technology, copper became available in far larger quantities, and new uses for it were rapidly found, both as tools, such as sickles, knives and awls, and as daggers and other weapons. The demand for ore grew and, as the surface deposits became exhausted, it was necessary to dig mines into the ground, pursuing the seams of ore as they snaked their way into the deep rocks of the Earth.

At Rudna Glava in eastern Serbia, mines were dug about 6500 years ago, and fires were lit beneath the seams of ore to open up cracks – the points of weakness which could then be exploited. The most effective tools were large stones with a groove carved around the centre, which formed a 'waist' around which a rope or leather thong could be tied. Gripping the other end of the rope in one hand, the miner, lying face down in the mine, swung the stone hard against the cracks in the metal-bearing seam, weakening it still further.

Finally, a piece of antler was used as a pick, to prise out lumps of ore. These were carried out of the mine, probably in baskets, and pounded to dust with the help of large grinding stones; impurities were then picked out before the ore was smelted. The smelting itself was probably done in a furnace or kiln, the copper emerging magically from the ore as glistening orange beads; the remainder was left as slag.

When these easily smelted ores were exhausted, the miners had to dig deeper or search in some other place. The ores that they next discovered and exploited contained some arsenic along with the copper – a fortuitous find, since the arsenic-copper alloy proved harder than pure copper. Soon these arsenical ores were themselves exhausted, and the metal-hungry societies of the Balkans moved on, this time to ores of copper sulphide which lay deeper in the ground.

In time, metalsmiths embarked

CAST IN THE PAST **Hammering was used for the earliest metals; the technique of pouring molten metal into a cast was discovered later. Casting was used to make this fine bronze palstave, found in London.**

on the experiments that led to the making of bronze, an alloy of copper and tin. Bronze is a little harder than copper, but it is far easier to cast in a mould. Moulds were made from pieces of stone, such as sandstone, carved into appropriate shapes, or sometimes from clay. The metal in its molten state was poured into the mould – a hazardous undertaking that must sometimes have ended with serious burns for those involved.

The invention of bronze coincides with a more widespread use of metal in certain parts of the world, which is why the first metal-using era is generally known as the Bronze Age rather than the Copper Age. Experiments with other metals continued, however, and in China about 4000 years ago, pure tin and pure lead were both used, as well as an alloy of tin and lead. Items made of these metals are found at the same archaeological sites as tools made of copper. Lead was occasionally used in south-west Asia as well, and gold and silver were used in jewellery in Mesopotamia from about 6000 years ago.

THE IRON AGE

The first objects made of iron appear just over 4000 years ago, but they are few and far between, and were clearly valued for their rarity. This is demonstrated by two ceremonial daggers from the tomb of the Egyptian prince Tutankhamun: one dagger has a gold blade, but the other has a blade of iron, suggesting that this was considered to be gold's equal in prestige value.

Smelting iron ore required a more delicate control of the chemical processes than that involved in the smelting of copper. The breakthrough came about 3200 years ago, and once techniques of iron-smelting and iron-working had become widespread, the new material proved far more valuable than

NATURAL RICHES **Native copper glints from this rock in Zambia. Early metalworkers in the Near East used local native copper, but supplies were soon exhausted, forcing them to smelt ores.**

IMPRESSIONS ON CLAY
Useful information has come from impressions made accidentally on clay, when newly made pots were placed on the ground and marked by whatever they rested on. Impressions of matting have been found on some pots; and occasionally there are signs of a grain of barley, sufficiently detailed for archaeologists to confirm that it was a cultivated type rather than a wild one.

---

bronze. This was partly due to its greater strength and hardness, but also to the fact that its ore was common throughout the world, whereas copper ores are scarce and ores of tin, the other ingredient of bronze, are similarly rare.

In some parts of the world, the advent of iron-working was associated with troubled times and with the need for weapons. This seems to have been the case around the Mediterranean and, to a lesser extent, in south-west Asia. By contrast, in prehistoric Thailand there was a relatively settled and peaceful society, and iron implements, like the bronze implements before them, were used mainly for digging up roots, harvesting rice, or cutting bamboo cane. This difference is reflected in the different technologies used by metalworkers in these regions. Whereas the metalworking of the Mediterranean moved more and more towards hard steel, containing a high proportion of carbon to give an extra edge against enemies, in Thailand a simpler technology continued for thousands of years, producing softer low-carbon steels.

THE AFRICAN IRON AGE
In Africa, to the south of the Sahara Desert, iron transformed the lives of both the people and the land. There had been no

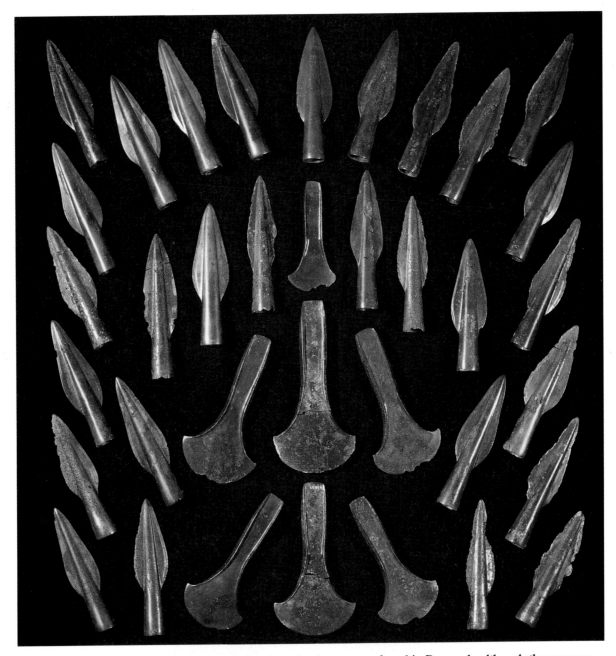

HIDDEN HOARD This hoard of bronze spearheads and palstaves was found in Denmark, although the weapons had all been made in Germany or Switzerland; they are about 3500 years old.

Bronze Age here, and iron was the first metal to be used – by a prehistoric people, known collectively as the Bantu speakers, who moved southwards.

The Bantu speakers had originated in West Africa, and spread south and east across the continent at surprising speed, between about 3000 and 2000 years ago. Their speedy progress was aided by their mastery of iron and by the effectiveness of iron axes against the hard timbers of the African forests. The Bantu speakers made a great contribution to crop-growing in areas that had formerly been forest, inhabited largely by hunter-gatherers such as the pygmies. In the parts of East Africa that were already occupied by farmers, the Bantu speakers' iron technology was simply absorbed into traditional patterns of life. As they moved on farther, into southern Africa, the Bantu speakers took over lands that had never been farmed before.

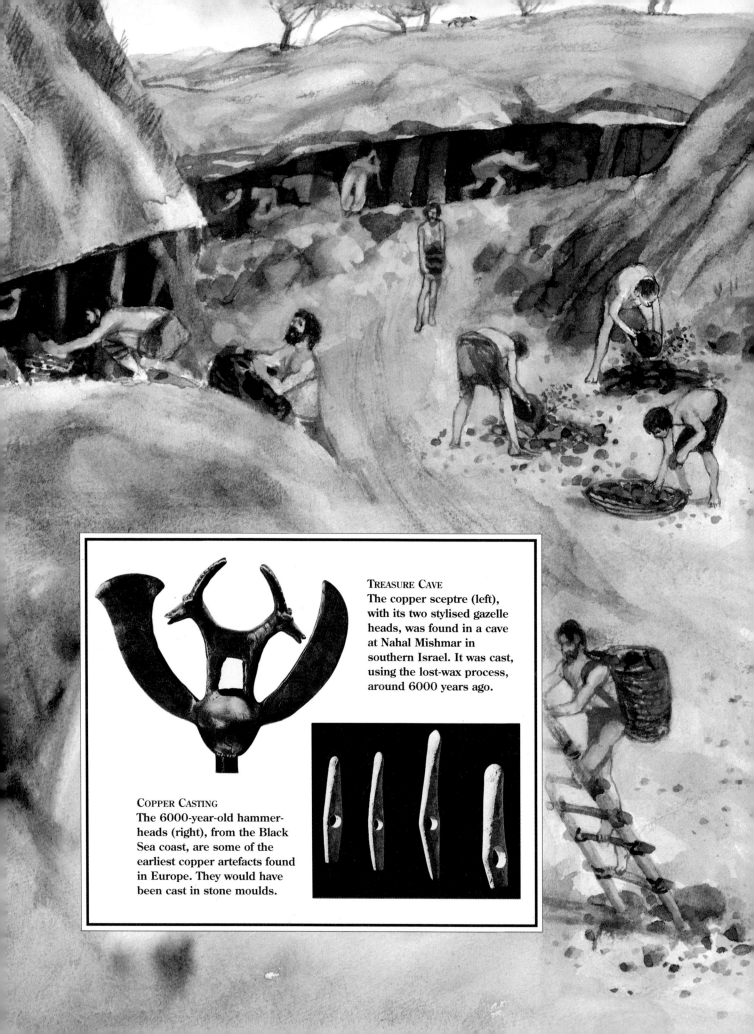

TREASURE CAVE
The copper sceptre (left),
with its two stylised gazelle
heads, was found in a cave
at Nahal Mishmar in
southern Israel. It was cast,
using the lost-wax process,
around 6000 years ago.

COPPER CASTING
The 6000-year-old hammer-
heads (right), from the Black
Sea coast, are some of the
earliest copper artefacts found
in Europe. They would have
been cast in stone moulds.

WORKING IN A COPPER MINE

ONE EARLY TECHNIQUE of mining copper was to use fire to heat the roof of the mine shaft (left). When the roof collapsed, the ore-bearing rocks could be brought up out of the shaft. The ore was then pounded into smaller fragments with stone hammers and heated in a furnace fired with charcoal (below) to 1100°C (2012°F). At this temperature, the liquid copper ran down the sloping floor at the base of the furnace and out of a tapping hole. The copper ingots produced in this way tended to be full of air bubbles, so they had to be remelted in a crucible to refine the metal. Impurities floated to the surface and were removed. The copper was then cast in a mould.

FROM HUNTING TO FARMING

From about 12 000 years ago, independently and in different parts of the world,

people started to shape nature to their own ends: sowing cereal crops and domesticating animals.

The invention of agriculture transformed not only their lifestyle but the landscape as well.

ON THE EDGE of the Congo forest in West Africa, two groups of people, the Bantu speaking farmers and the Baka Pygmies, live alongside one another in an uneasy coexistence. Their whole approach to the problem of obtaining food is fundamentally different, and this is what makes them interesting to anyone trying to reconstruct the past. They demonstrate vividly the huge change in patterns of everyday life that occurred when prehistoric people switched from hunting and gathering to farming. The Baka Pygmy is by nature a nomadic forest-dweller, who stalks noiselessly between the trees in pursuit of antelopes and elephants. He also catches fish and small crocodiles in the forest streams, collects termites and fruit, and takes honey from the nests of wild bees high up in hollow tree trunks. The Bantu speaker is a farmer, tilling land on the edge of the forest. His plots consist of small fields that were once forested but whose trees were felled long ago by the first African farmers. Like those distant ancestors, the modern Bantu farmer lives by raising goats and chickens for their meat, and by growing cereal crops such as millet and sorghum.

One is an adaptable opportunist who fits in with nature, while the other seeks to shape nature so that it serves human ends. The Pygmy, armed with time-honoured knowledge of the jungle and the cunning of a lifelong hunter, trusts that the natural products of the forest can always be found in sufficient quantities to fend off hunger. The Bantu, by contrast, imposes a particular kind of vegetation on the land, rigidly controls what grows, keeps plant-eating insects and birds away as much as possible, and then takes all or most of the land's produce.

EARLY HUNTER   In a rock painting from Natal, South Africa, an armed hunter pursues wild game.

Not surprisingly, nomadic Pygmies require far more land per head; they also share this land with a far greater variety of plants and animals. They eat a more varied diet and do not need to work as hard as the Bantu – a few hours a day are all that is needed to collect enough food. On the other hand, they do not have the option of working harder and thus dramatically increasing their food supply, because there are limits to the total amount of food available in the forest.

Although the Bantu despise the Pygmies and call them 'primitive', their villages are less healthy than the Pygmies' forest encampments, because a high concentration of people living permanently in one place pollutes water supplies and encourages contagious diseases. The Bantu have more food available most of the time than the Pygmies, but they have to work very hard for it. Theirs is backbreaking labour, as they dig and hoe the hard, sun-baked soil or pull up the weeds that threaten to choke the crops. For

THE USEFUL GAZELLE

Gazelles were probably domesticated, or partially domesticated, in the Near East, before sheep and goats became the main domesticated animals. At a cave site, known as Nahal Oren, on Mount Carmel in Israel, gazelles accounted for 80 per cent of all meat eaten, and more than half of the animals killed were young. Youth is a characteristic feature of the remains of domestic herds, whereas among wild animals killed by hunters there is a much wider age range.

SUCCESSFUL HUNT In the settled phase that preceded the invention of agriculture, wild animals and plants still provided all the food for villagers in the Near East. But an increasing reliance on the seeds of wild grasses pointed the way forwards, towards the domestication of cereal crops.

all this effort they are rewarded with a monotonous starchy diet, and sometimes they suffer crop failures. In times of shortage, it is the Bantu who rely on the Pygmies for meat supplies, trading paraffin or cloth for freshly killed forest antelope. There is also far more tension and unrest in the Bantu villages than among the Pygmies, who can resolve problems by splitting into smaller bands and moving on, thus separating warring parties.

AN ANCIENT LIFESTYLE

The Pygmies demonstrate just how viable – and indeed easy – the ancient hunter-gatherer way of life was. Fifteen thousand years ago everyone lived this way, regardless of climate or vegetation. Hunter-gatherers could thrive in the ice-bound

lands of the Arctic as well as in the tropics. They made a living not only in the forests, but also on the open grassy plains, along the seashore, by lakes and rivers, on mountain slopes and even in deserts. Exactly why anyone should have made the switch to farming, given the extra effort required and the many drawbacks, is a difficult question to answer. But the transition did occur in several different parts of the world between about 12 000 years and 5000 years ago. The fact that it happened quite independently in both the Old World and the New suggests that there was some driving force behind the invention of agriculture, although we do not yet understand fully what this was.

One fact is clear, however. After the transition had been made it was hard to go back, because the

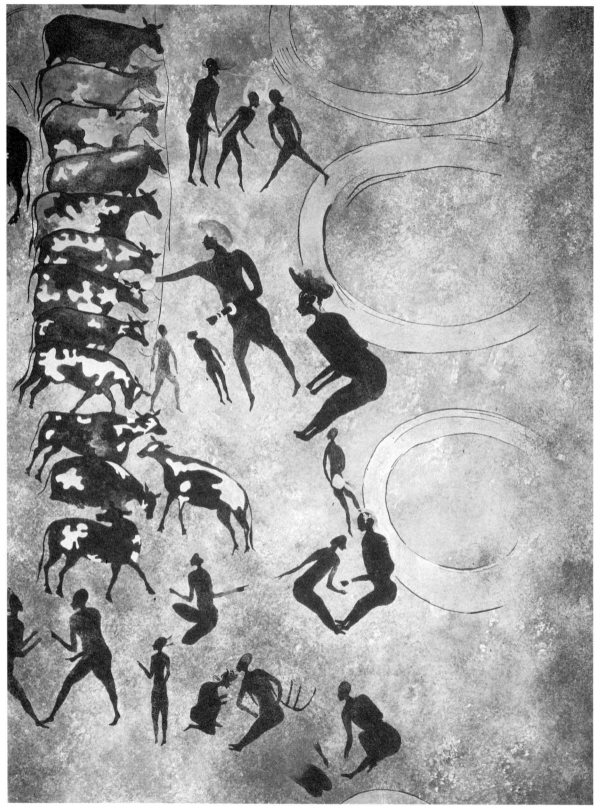

FARMED ANIMALS In a cave painting from the Sahara of about 2000 BC, herders arrive at a market where animals are exchanged, bargains struck, and a disagreement is settled by violent means (bottom left).

EXPERIMENTAL FARMING AND STRESSFUL TIMES

HARDSHIP LINES Seasonal food shortages caused 'Harris lines' across the bones of early farmers, as in the human tibia, or shin bone, above.

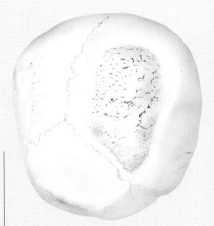

SKULL DEFECT The pitted surface – a sign of osteoporosis – exhibited by a skull from the Nazca area of Peru is thought to have been the result of vitamin deficiencies.

AS PREHISTORIC PEOPLE began to experiment with farming, new threats to their health emerged. The bones of people from Paloma in Peru, about 10 000 years ago, show distinctive lines when X-rayed – a sign of arrested growth which suggests stressful times. These lines seem to mark the coming each year of times when food was short, and occur in people who lived when agriculture was just beginning. Once farming techniques were established and food supplies assured, these lines are no longer found in skeletons. People also grew taller than before, and their life expectancy increased as they became better at growing crops and storing them for hard times.

human population increased within farming areas once there was extra food available and people were settled in permanent villages. Nomadic hunter-gatherers, on the other hand, have smaller families – something that is achieved, in part, by breast-feeding each child for up to four years, which suppresses conception. Having to carry babies from place to place encourages nomadic mothers to maintain practices such as this, which space out their children so that there is never more than one infant at a time who needs carrying.

PREHISTORIC PARASITES

Research into parasites has helped to identify aspects of prehistoric diet. The eggs of a tapeworm, which spends part of its life cycle in fish, have been found in human coprolites – fossilised faeces – on the coast of Chile. People here must have eaten uncooked or partly cured fish. And the recovery of the eggs of another tapeworm, which spends part of its life in grain-eating rodents, indicates that people in the south-western USA stored grain.

The first settled farmers passed a point of no return – without anyone realising at the time that it was happening. From then on, farming was the only way the extra mouths could be fed, unless there was a large area of productive uninhabited terrain into which to expand – which there rarely was. Consequently, prehistoric farmers were forced to continue with the agricultural way of life, even when insect pests and plant diseases started to destroy the crops, whose very availability had caused them to flourish. Such problems must have made the life of early farmers more and more difficult, and there may have been crop failures and famines when pests or diseases struck. But for most people, there was no going back to hunting and gathering because of the increased population density.

SETTLED HUNTER-GATHERERS

There are some exceptions to the generalisation that hunter-gatherers are nomadic while farmers are sedentary. If natural foodstuffs are available in unusual abundance, then hunter-gatherers may settle down in one spot. At a certain phase in prehistory, from about 12 500 years ago in the Near

East, such a lifestyle became more common than ever before or since. Some of these settled hunter-gatherers may have formed the basis of later farming communities.

SHELL MOUNDS

The end of the last ice age spelled the end of a way of life: the heroic pursuit of large game animals such as mammoth and bison, and the relatively affluent lifestyle it had permitted. As the climate warmed up and tree growth returned, large game arrivals either died out or became elusive forest-dwellers which were more difficult to hunt. At the same time, sea levels rose all around the world and, while this created problems, in time it also offered new opportunities. What had once been shorelines now became seabeds, which were extremely fertile because the rotting detritus left by previous human encampments along the former coast, as well as sea-bird colonies and coastal plants, created a supply of nutrients in the water. As temperatures rose, these waters began to teem with life, including shellfish such as mussels, oysters and scallops. Shellfish could easily be collected at low tide by the humans of post-glacial times. Plentiful and rich in protein, they became the staple diet of quite a few human communities around the world.

GOAT VERSUS GAZELLE

Goats became more popular domesticated animals with early farmers because they ate a wider range of plant foods than gazelles and were easier to keep. Goats can chew their way through hard woody twigs, and so they were used to clear scrub vegetation before land was planted with crops. Hard stubble left after the cereals had been harvested also provided goats with food – and if there was surplus grain at the end of winter, this too could be fed to the goats.

Such communities have left their mark in the form of shell mounds, the accumulated after-dinner debris from hundreds, or even thousands, of years of occupation. Huge piles of ancient shells have been found by excavators in the Americas, especially along the coasts of Florida, in various parts of Europe, notably Denmark, and in the Far East. Japan has some of the largest mounds, and at some sites these actually enclose whole villages, the mound being built up in a horseshoe shape with about a dozen small pit-houses arranged in an arc around the edge of the enclosed space, and an open plaza in the centre.

RUBBISH DUMP   Over the millennia, a prehistoric shell mound – the leftovers of a seaside community that once feasted on shellfish – has migrated miles inland, as a result of changing sea levels.

A CONDEMNED MAN FROM TOLLUND

HE IS KNOWN AS TOLLUND MAN, a leathery brown corpse from a peat bog in northern Denmark, almost perfectly preserved by the acid waters of the bog – so well preserved that he was first thought to have died only a decade or so before. Radiocarbon dating revealed him to be 2000 years old. His ancestors had farmed the rich peaty soil of the locality for at least 4000 years, and his technology and lifestyle were relatively sophisticated – his people used iron tools to till the soil and lived in substantial wood-framed houses. But, as Tollund Man has revealed, they still collected wild plant seeds for food.

Tollund Man was killed, probably by his fellow villagers. They put a noose around his neck and pulled it tight from behind. Then they threw the lifeless body into the bog. Whether he was a sacrifice to the gods or a criminal who was executed, we will never know.

SKULLCAP **Tollund Man's leathery head and sheepskin cap were preserved in the peaty soil.**

At least 12 hours before he was put to death, Tollund Man was given a last meal, a thin gruel made from barley and linseed grains, together with the seeds of several wild plants: knotweed and a cabbage-like weed known as 'gold-of-pleasure', dock, camomile, black bindweed and bristle-grass. This pottage has been re-created using the same seeds, and proved immensely unappetising.

Were these wild seeds regularly gathered for food, or was the meal given to Tollund Man an unusual one for the time? It has been suggested that, if he was a sacrifice to the gods, he could have been given a special meal whose ingredients were of ritual significance. More probably, he was a condemned man being given the equivalent of bread-and-water: the cheapest food currently available.

What is intriguing for archaeologists is the discovery that, even after thousands of years of agriculture, people were still using wild plants as a basic source of calories. It had been expected that they would collect fruit and nuts from the wild, as we still pick blackberries and hazelnuts, but that agricultural produce would be their main source of nourishment.

Studies of the remains in such shell mounds reveal that the ancient Japanese shellfish-eaters were living in these villages all year round: they had abandoned nomadism for permanent settlements. Besides the shellfish, they benefited from the sea in other ways, catching fish and hunting seals and sea lions. Minute traces of dolphin oil, identified on fragments of cooking pots by chemical analysis, show that people also ate these marine mammals. Dugout canoes found buried in the shell mounds reveal that they could fish and hunt at sea, rather than relying solely on stranded prey. When winter made such foods unavailable, hunting expeditions went inland in search of deer and wild pigs. Chestnuts, acorns and berries were eaten in the autumn and some stored for winter, while in spring the tender young fronds of ferns were added to the menu.

Recent evidence suggests that some of the settled hunter-gatherers of ancient Japan started growing crops in a small way. They did so on their own initiative, using local plants, and they provide us with one of the clearest pictures available from the archaeological record of a community immediately before – and after – the invention of farming. The plants they chose to grow were a wild grass which eventually became the crop now known as barnyard millet, and a leafy plant now called beefsteak herb. These crops made up a minor part of their diet – a small addition to what could be collected or killed in the wild. Perhaps they were added to the diet for nutritional reasons, the hunters knowing instinctively that they needed more greenstuff in their oily protein-rich diet. If edible green plants were scarce, this may have spurred the cultivation of certain specimens. Only later were crops such as barley, rice and millet introduced into Japan from China, along with a whole new way of life, committed to full-time agriculture.

The invention of farming in Japan was a relatively late development, about 5000 years ago. By then agriculture was well established in large parts of south-west Asia, in many regions of the Far East, in Central America, and in the mountains and coastal regions of what is now Peru. In most of these areas, agriculture had been an original invention, probably made by settled hunter-gatherers, who took local wild plants and began growing them as crops.

THE FIRST FARMERS

The world's first farming communities arose some 9000 years ago in the Near East – the oldest site discovered so far is at a site called Aswad near present-day Damascus. Agriculture was not a sudden development here. People had already been living in the locality for a full 9000 years, surviving as hunter-gatherers in what was then an open landscape of tall waving grass, with scattered trees such as evergreen oaks, pistachios and wild apricots. As well as collecting nuts and fruits, the people of Aswad gathered the seeds of wild grasses for food. They relied heavily on such seeds, eventually making them the mainstay of their diet.

Another site several hundred miles to the south tells much the same story. Along the peaceful shores of the sea of Galilee, then much greener and cooler than today, the charred remains of grass seeds have been found at an excavation known as Ohalo 2. Along with these burned grass

seeds are those of wild lupins, which are similar to peas or lentils – they would have lent extra protein to the diet. It is clear, however, that the grasses were the principal source of food for the people of Ohalo 2, and that grass seeds were available in great abundance.

Ohalo 2 has also yielded pestles and mortars made of limestone, that may have been used to grind the grass seeds and turn them into flour. This could then have been baked into bread. If such bread was made, it would have been a flat bread rolled out on a slab and then cooked on a large flat stone taken red-hot from the fire. The end product would have been similar to the pitta bread or *nan* bread of today – delicious if eaten hot from the cooking stone. Alternatively, the grass seeds could simply have been roasted and eaten whole. Finding pestles and mortars is not a sure sign that flour or bread was made. Pestles could have been used to grind acorns which are also a nutritious food, or to pulverise red ochre for painting.

Whichever way they were prepared, these wild grasses were obviously a staple food for the people of the time. Although still living as hunter-gatherers,

PRODUCTIVE LANDSCAPE The intensively farmed land near Quanzhou in China has probably been under cultivation for several thousand years. The first farmers transformed not only their own lives, but also the world around them.

they may well have been settled rather than no-madic, because they built houses of stone which might imply a certain permanence. If the people of Aswad and Ohalo 2 really were living a sedentary lifestyle, they must have had a reliable and sustaining source of food, comparable to the shellfish which allowed hunter-gatherers to settle in coastal regions of Japan, Denmark and elsewhere in the world. We can deduce from this that the grasses growing in the Near East 18 000 years ago were extremely productive and nutritious.

NEW PLANTS, NEW PEOPLE

When exactly these people changed from simply gathering wild grass seeds to deliberately planting them can never be pinpointed. The only firm evidence for the earliest agriculture comes in a change in the grasses themselves, because people are – intentionally or not – selecting particular kinds to plant and rejecting others.

The most useful characteristic that the earliest farmers could have hoped to develop in the wild grasses was a seedhead which did not shed its seeds as soon as they were ripe – instead it held on to them, making the job of harvesting far easier and less wasteful. Once people began saving seed to sow the following year, this characteristic almost certainly 'selected itself', because a mutant plant which retained its seeds (wild grasses throw up such mutants occasionally) would always contribute all its seeds to the harvest, whereas other plants would sometimes contribute no seeds at all, or only a proportion of their seeds. When the seeds from one harvest were resown the next year, the percentage from seed-retaining mutant plants would have increased marginally and, with this process being repeated over the centuries, the mutant plants would have gradually become more common.

EARLY CROP Emmer wheat, a primitive, slender-eared variety, has long bristles not seen on modern wheat.

DOMESTIC TRADITION An African woman of prehistoric times uses a stone to pound seeds in a hollow made in a much larger stone. This method is still in use in parts of Africa today.

To the inhabitants of the Near East, gathering grass seeds into their baskets on a sunny day in late summer, and trying not to allow too many of them to fall to the earth, the advantages of the mutant plants whose seedheads remained intact would have been obvious. But before they could realise this, the mutant plants had to have become common enough to be noticed. Geneticists estimate that it took about 1000 years for the mutants to form a noticeable proportion of ordinary plants.

Once this had happened, the selection process soon became deliberate, with the novel seeds being picked out for planting. Within a few hundred years, the early farmers had created cereal crops in which all the plants held the seeds fast and never shed them. By 9000 years ago, when such seedheads appear for the first time in the archaeological record, farming must already have been well established.

SOWING SEEDS

It was a very distant ancestor of these Near Eastern farmers – a person living much more than 10 000 years ago – who had made the crucial decision to sow seeds in order to boost the supply of wild grasses. What could possibly have led to that decision? A change of climate is often proposed as a trigger factor, but the evidence about climate in the

FLINT REAPER Ancient sickles used the natural curve of an animal's jawbone, made sharp with tiny chipped flints set into the inner edge.

The realisation that seeds would sprout and grow into new plants was obviously a crucial factor. It is something that we take for granted, having been taught it from childhood, but for the people of prehistory it was far from obvious, and a discovery that they had to make for themselves. Perhaps the discovery came when seeds that had been stored for the winter were accidentally spilled on the ground, only to sprout and grow into new plants the following year. Or perhaps some seeds were scattered over the bare ground as part of a religious ceremony, and when these later germinated and grew, the possibilities of planting them deliberately became apparent.

FERTILE CRESCENT

At a site known as Abu Hureya alongside the Euphrates river in northern Syria, we have a more rounded picture of what people were eating during the earliest agricultural phase. Grass seeds, whether from wild plants or cultivated ones, were the cornerstone of the diet, but although the populace relied heavily on this starchy staple, they were still hunter-gatherers at heart, and they regularly picked other wild plant foods beside grasses, including pistachio nuts and wild lentils. They also hunted small game such as rabbits, gazelles and the wild ancestors of sheep and goats. In the waters of the Euphrates, they caught fish and freshwater mussels, all of which supplemented their staple diet of grass seeds with some much-needed protein.

It is tempting to think of them combining these tasty ingredients in appetising recipes, but we have no way of knowing if they did so, or if cookery was still to be invented. Most hunter-gatherers simply eat what they find, sometimes grinding, cooking or soaking foods to make them more appetising, but without any concerted attempt to combine different foods or to modify flavours.

Near East during this period is inconclusive. Some of it suggests that the weather got colder and wetter, or that the rising sea levels which occurred at the end of the last ice age may have reduced the living space of the human population. Changes such as these could have made life more difficult by limiting food supplies, and this in turn could have led to the idea of deliberately nurturing food plants rather than relying on nature to provide them.

There may well have been other innovations, too, that led to this crucial change. Perhaps people were already in the habit of cutting back small trees that invaded the grassy areas, so that the grasses would not suffer too much competition. Fire might also have been used to knock back the growth of scrub and trees, encouraging the survival and spread of the grasses. Measures such as these, which we know have been practised by hunter-gatherers living in savannah or prairie in the recent past, could have paved the way for true agriculture in the Near East.

Once this practice of farming had become established in certain areas, it spread rapidly through the rest of the Fertile Crescent, a huge tract of land which runs northwards through the present-day lands of Israel, Jordan and Syria, east through Turkey and south-eastwards into Iraq. The fertile lands of this zone are fed by rivers running down from the mountains to the north.

Ancient farming settlements have been found throughout the Fertile Crescent, including the famous city of Jericho and the Mesopotamian towns of Uruk and Ur, which later developed into powerful city-states. True wheat and barley were first grown in the villages of the Fertile Crescent – domesticated descendants of the wild grasses that had fed previous generations. It was here, too, that the sickle was invented, first to cut grass stems for thatching the roofs of houses, and later deployed to harvest wild grass seeds. It finally became the essential tool of farmers harvesting cereal crops. The jawbone of an animal would be transformed into a sickle by setting tiny pieces of sharpened flint into the slots where the teeth had been, a laborious task given the time needed to make each of the miniature blades made of flint.

Keeping sheep and goats as domestic animals was a later development, which reduced the need for

HARVEST TIME Early farmers, in what is now Hungary, made this clay figure, shown holding a sickle.

WOMAN'S BEST FRIEND A 12 000-year-old burial found in Israel contained the skeleton of a very old person, probably a woman, buried with her left hand and head resting on a puppy. Evidence suggests that the young animal was domesticated.

hunting, although wild animals were undoubtedly caught as well. Perhaps people took to capturing and controlling animals because the stocks of wild game were running low, or there could have been more subtle psychological reasons, prompting people who now had mastery over plants to seek a similar mastery of the animal kingdom.

DOMESTICATING ANIMALS
Whatever the reason, there were both major gains and major losses involved in keeping domestic animals. On the positive side, farmers now had the means to care for their soil: the manure of the animals could be used to fertilise the fields, whose natural fertility would undoubtedly have begun to decline after several centuries of cropping. On the negative side, domesticated animals introduced new diseases to the human population, although the fact that infections were derived from the herds may not have been obvious at the time.

Rearing animals also demanded far more work from the early farmers: they had to be guarded from danger, herded to green pastures, supplied with water, and cared for when sick. Unlike modern farm animals which have had millennia of breeding for passivity, the sheep and goats of the first farmers were still half-wild. These creatures of uncertain temper and strong will were liable to wander off if left untended, or to lash out with hooves and horns at their human owners. In choosing the animals to breed from, the early farmers would have first selected the most biddable and placid of their flock, so that in time the problem of managing them would be reduced.

THE SPREAD OF FARMING
Within a few thousand years of its invention, agriculture had spread from the Fertile Crescent into what is now western Turkey, and moved eastwards as far as Pakistan. It had stimulated the development of larger and larger settlements, including one of the first walled cities, ancient Jericho, which was defended by a perimeter wall 10 ft (3 m) thick

EMBATTLED FARMERS The massive walls and tall lookout tower of Jericho testify to the conflict and theft that were one outcome of agriculture. The security of storing food had turned into the anxiety of attracting ruthless enemies.

millet, while cabbages and plums were also grown. Much later, soya beans, wheat, rice and sorghum were also adopted in east Asia. The wheat had been domesticated in the Near East, and the sorghum in West Africa south of the Sahara. Both were brought to China by migrants or traders. The long-distance movement of cultivated plants shows just how valuable they were to the very early farmers.

In the same way, agriculture moved southwards from China into the lands of South-east Asia. At the cave known as Bui Ceri Uato, on the island of East Timor, there are layers indicating human occupation that span a period of 6000 years. The lowest layers contain stone tools and the bones of snakes, lizards, fruit bats and giant rats, all used for food. Mixed in with these tools and bones are shells, the remains of shellfish gathered on the nearby coral reefs and mangrove swamps. Some of the shells had been fashioned into fish-hooks or beads.

About 5000 years ago, when the cave had already been occupied for 5000 years, the bones of pigs and fragments of pottery suddenly appear on the floor of the cave. Pottery is generally associated with farmers, and there seems little doubt that both pigs and pots were introduced by farming people from the north. Many more stone tools are found in the upper layers, along with evidence that yams, rice and other crops were being grown.

One interesting discovery from South-east Asia is that the betel nut was being grown at an early stage, along with a pepper plant whose seeds are still chewed locally, to produce a narcotic effect.

and had a stone lookout tower that stood some 30 ft (9 m) high.

The heavy fortifications of Jericho indicate some of the problems that came with greater prosperity. Stores of grain laid up for the winter were a great temptation to outsiders. Such food could be stolen by raiding parties, as could herds of domestic animals. The accumulation of food was a trigger for aggression and raiding, such as hunter-gatherers of previous generations had never known.

FARMING IN THE FAR EAST

Farming began in northern China about 8000 years ago and may, once again, have been a completely independent development. Local grasses were domesticated to become foxtail millet and broomcorn

FERTILITY CULTS The bull shrines found in farming settlements such as Çatal Hüyük, now in Turkey, suggest a fertility cult. Perhaps offerings were made to ensure a good harvest, or to give thanks.

Even the earliest farmers grew plants purely for their value as a drug (the betel nut has no nutritional value).

From South-east Asia, farming spread across the Pacific in the canoes of the earliest colonisers, finally reaching Easter Island and New Zealand. Once farming people began to travel in this way, they were forced to adapt their agricultural techniques to new and very different conditions. This often involved changing the way they grew the crops they had brought with them, or it could lead to the adoption of new crops more suited to the new terrain, as

happened in the cool damp climate of New Zealand where the crops of South-east Asia and the Pacific were never truly at home and where they grew yam, taro and sweet potato instead.

FARMING IN EUROPE

A similar process occurred in Europe, where farming arrived slowly, beginning about 7000 years ago in the south of France and reaching Britain about 6000 years ago. The crops grown were wheat and barley which had originated in the Near East. During the slow move northwards, these plants were gradually modified to suit their new and much cooler environment. Domesticated animals were also brought in, but the goat, so hardy in the warmer zones around the Mediterranean, was less well suited to cooler northern climates.

Exactly how crops and farming techniques were brought into Europe is a matter of great debate. Were there influxes of farming peoples, bringing their strange new way of life with them and taking over lands that had previously been uninhabited or in use by hunter-gatherers? Or was it that ideas and crops travelled northwards along established trade routes with enterprising groups of hunter-gatherers trying them out, and slowly abandoning their former nomadic way of life? These are questions that archaeologists are still attempting to answer.

FARMERS OF THE HILLS AND VALLEYS

PEOPLE living in the Vindhya Range, a chain of hills in northern India, probably stumbled on agriculture quite independently of their counterparts, the early farmers of the Near East.

Rice was the staple crop here, and its cultivation began more than 7000 years ago. What was unusual about the farmers of the western Vindhya hills, however, is that, unlike other very early agriculturalists who tended to settle in one place, they farmed two quite separate areas, taking advantage of the different growing conditions.

They seem to have spent part of the year down on the flood plains of the River Ganges, where the exceptionally fertile soil threw up an abundant crop of rice.

Then, having harvested this grain, the migrant farmers carried it back with them into the hills.

GOOD LIFE At Butser Farm in southern England, archaeologists re-create the farming methods of 5000 years ago.

The fact that agriculture spread with other items, such as pottery, encouraged archaeologists of the past to believe that it was the farming people themselves who were travelling northwards, displacing or conquering the hunter-gatherers. Today there is less certainty about such events. Many archaeologists now believe that it was a movement of knowledge, implements and seeds – the raw materials of agriculture – that spread northwards, not the farmers themselves.

AGRICULTURE IN THE AMERICAS

According to a legend of the Maya people of Central America, the gods made the first human beings out of maize. This cereal crop, so different in appearance from the wheat, barley and rice of the Old World, was domesticated in the uplands of what is now Mexico more than 8000 years ago. It soon

THE REVERED BEAN

Cocoa was first grown in Central America. To the Aztecs it was a sacred potion, reserved for the emperor and nobles, and drunk without sugar or milk, a strong and bitter brew. Cocoa beans were also used as money.

became an indispensable foodstuff, the staple diet on which the great kingdoms of the Aztecs and the Maya were built. Its extraordinary importance is indicated by the many maize legends that exist and by the pots and other artefacts fashioned in the shape of a maize cob.

Other crops domesticated in Central America included the sweet pepper, chilli pepper, haricot beans, avocados, pumpkins and squashes. Very few animals were domesticated here – only the turkey, the muscovy duck and the stingless bee.

Maize was carried southwards, and eventually reached the Andes where it was grown alongside locally domesticated crops such as the potato, lima bean, quinoa grain and sweet potato.

Andean farmers, in time, domesticated several animals. Llamas were kept not only for their meat but also for leather and wool, and their fat was burned to give light. They were, in addition, sturdy beasts of burden that could tackle the steep paths of the high Andes even when heavily laden. The guanaco and the alpaca were kept mainly for their wool. These mountain animals did not spread beyond the Andes to any great extent because they were ill-adapted to other climates. One of the most curious of all domesticated animals, the guinea pig, also originated in the high Andes. These small

117

creatures provided a substantial amount of meat in some Andean regions.

The art of farming travelled northwards from Mexico and Central America into some parts of North America, where the native people grew crops such as maize, beans, squash and tobacco. A few crops were domesticated locally, such as the sunflower, brought into cultivation about 4000 years ago in parts of what are now Kentucky and Missouri. As the farming tradition moved northwards, the tropical crop plants had to be adapted to cooler conditions and a shorter growing season. When the early Amerindian farmers of the north, such as the Iroquois, chose seeds to sow for the following season, they would have bred new strains from the original crops, and ones that were better suited to local conditions.

FARMING THE FORESTS
Early experiments in farming were mostly carried out in landscapes that were relatively open rather than heavily forested, often on grassy plains or high plateaus. In general, the very first farmers and their descendants worked the same land for centuries. In the tropical jungles a different type of agriculture arose. Known as shifting cultivation or slash-and-burn, this method is so successful in dense forest that it is still practised in regions such as the Amazon Basin and South-east Asia, offering us a unique glimpse of a farming technique that has survived from prehistory.

RODENTS FOR ROASTING A 'stirrup pot', with a handle that also served as a spout, shows a guinea pig, the smallest domesticated mammal. The animal was domesticated by pre-Inca civilisations in Peru, and was allowed to scurry about the houses, feeding on scraps.

Shifting cultivators exploit land for a period of two to four years, sometimes longer. Then, when the weeds become too numerous or aggressive to be hacked back any longer, the farmer moves on – sometimes just a short distance, sometimes many miles – chooses a new plot in the forest, clears it and starts afresh. Trees on a new plot are usually ringed first, a cut being made in the bark all the way round so that the lifelines of water and sap can no longer flow. This kills the tree and, once it has dried out, it becomes much easier to burn. A season or so after the trees have been ringed, the plot is fired.

FIRE AND FARMING
The blaze is carefully controlled, and its consequences planned in order to maximise conditions for crop growth. The ashes from the burned trees provide minerals which fertilise the soil. Vines and other potentially troublesome weeds are destroyed along with their seeds. Some trees are felled before burning and allowed to lie crisscrossed on the scorched earth, in order to reduce soil erosion. When all is ready, crop seeds are sown, and the young plants carefully tended as the green shoots poke up through the blackened earth.

Fire is a tool that any farmer can use. Settled farmers, however, who expect to stay in one place for several generations at least, must use it with restraint. Farmers living on the open plains may well have fired the land regularly to clear it of scrub and young trees. But gradually, as the population of the world grew and as the amount of fertile land available for farming decreased, the use of fire as a land-management tool probably declined. Settled farmers realised that they had to be more careful with the land and had to maintain the fertility of the soil.

Whereas the shifting cultivator can move on when the soil becomes impoverished, the settled farmer must renew its vital nutrients. For the settled farmer, digging in weeds or adding manure has the advantage of enriching the soil and improving its texture. Yet burning still has a role to play, especially in clearing the land of troublesome

TRADITIONAL LIFE The Masai of East Africa are herders whose agricultural wealth lies not in land but in animals.

weeds, or in killing off insect pests and fungi that must be eliminated before the next crop is sown.

There is no sharp dividing line between shifting cultivators and settled cultivators today. Most farming people who live in regions where there is some spare land available will move on eventually, even if they spend several generations in the same spot. Shifting cultivators, on the other hand, often migrate in a huge circle and wind up where they had started within a timespan of some 50 years. As

a result, they may be considered, effectively, as 'settled' as the settled cultivators. We can guess that the same blurring of the boundaries occurred among prehistoric farmers.

HERDERS OF ANIMALS

The threat of raids by nomadic 'barbarians' is one that has haunted farmers in many parts of the world for thousands of years. It appears repeatedly in the earliest legends and written histories, and probably figured large in the lives of prehistoric farmers. The much-feared attackers were people known as pastoralists, who lived by herding cattle or horses, camels or goats. These people were (and are) farmers-on-the-move, their wealth and sense of identity invested, not in the land, but in the animals they cherished and defended – a form of uniquely mobile wealth.

To pastoralists, the herds are everything: their inherited wealth, their livelihood, their mode of transport and their next meal. Because the animals mean so much, and because they are always at risk from predators, pastoralists are ferocious in their defence. Present-day nomadic herdsmen, whether

THE HARDY POTATO

Potatoes were first domesticated high up in the Andes, on the bleak windswept altiplano around Lake Titicaca. They need fewer sunny frost-free days than grain crops (such as maize) to produce a ripe, edible harvest. Andean farmers found that they could preserve potatoes for the winter by taking advantage of the dry icy winds on the altiplano to 'freeze-dry' them. Freeze-dried potatoes, known as *chuño*, could be dipped into soup and eaten directly.

the Masai of East Africa or the Mongols of Central Asia, are invariably fierce warriors. The evidence of prehistory suggests that this necessary toughness could easily develop into a warring culture. Not all the nomadic pastoralists raided their more settled neighbours, but the temptation of their richly stocked granaries was strong.

ON THE MOVE

The question of how the nomadic lifestyle of the pastoralists originated is a difficult one. In Europe and Asia, it apparently developed from a more sedentary type of farming, involving crop growing and animal husbandry. Exactly why and when some of these settled farmers abandoned their fields and became nomadic herders is not yet known. What is clear is that once these roaming tribes evolved, they soon began to have an impact on those communities that stayed settled. The risk to the grain stores and to the herds of the farming villages led to more fortifications. Threats from the nomads may also have encouraged people to huddle together in larger settlements, which could have contributed to the growth of the first cities.

Not all nomadic pastoralists developed from communities of settled farmers. In the north of Scandinavia, people known as Sami or Lapps have a close relationship with reindeer herds on which they depend for meat, hides and other products. The herds are not, strictly speaking, domesticated, but they are partially under the control of the Sami.

Following the herds closely on their sledges, the Sami predict and sometimes to a limited extent control the movement of the reindeer. They are not herders, however. When they cannot easily keep up with the reindeer, as the animals go through a narrow gap or over steep rocky terrain, the Sami may take another route and intercept them later, knowing in advance which way the herd will go.

When the time comes for some reindeer to be killed, a tame animal is used to act as a decoy and to lure the chosen animals into a pen for slaughter. Tamed and castrated reindeer are also used to pull their sledges. The same degree of control over the reindeer herds is seen among certain tribes with a similar lifestyle living in parts of Siberia – other Siberian tribes again control the herds much less and are more like true hunters. There are also Siberian tribes whose reindeer are so tightly controlled that they are very much like domesticated animals, with the females even consenting to be milked. These different tribes show very clearly how some forms of pastoralism could have developed directly from hunting.

WILD AT HEART   The Sami (Lapps) tame a few reindeer and use them to draw sledges, but most of the herd remains wild – at least in temperament.

FROM SURVIVAL TO CIVILISATION

The desire to know and understand the Universe,

the richness and mystery of the imagination, the longing to

beautify, build stone monuments, elaborate and mythologise –

all these traits, which we recognise as particularly human, developed

in the course of prehistory, and pushed our species beyond the

boundaries of mere survival towards the first civilisations.

THE FIRST CITIES

With the appearance of the first city-states, beautiful and

elaborate goods were made, and stupendous monuments built, but the freedom

and leisure of most individuals was sharply curtailed.

ALL THAT REMAINS of the city of Ur is the ghostly ziggurat, a massive steep-sided brick-clad platform, three storeys high, which towers over the dry empty plains of Mesopotamia, silent and ominous. If a clock could be turned back 4000 years, the ziggurat would be decorated with colourful mosaics and planted with trees, while all around it stand a complex of ornate temples, tombs and palaces, where priests and rulers worship the moon god Nanna, to whom Ur was dedicated. Beyond these imposing public buildings stood the substantial three-storeyed mud-brick houses of the city-dwellers – people whom we now know as Sumerians – which stretched as far as the city wall, and some way beyond. On the edges of the city were two artificial harbours connected to the River

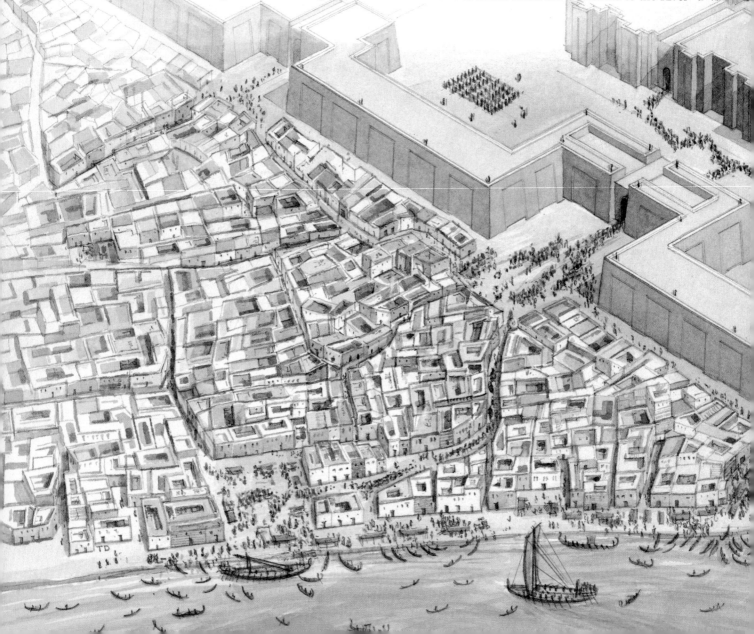

EARLY CITY This is how Ur may have looked about 4000 years ago. The ziggurat of the temple dominates the city centre. The River Euphrates runs around a part of the city's surrounding wall and is linked by canal to two harbours, one to the west, and one to the north.

Euphrates by a canal. There may also have been a shallow lagoon, for the sea level was higher then, and legend speaks of Ur being close to the sea.

The narrow, unpaved thoroughfares of the great city would have been crowded and busy as farmers arrived, driving their oxen to the temple. Traders riding mules, dusty and tired from their long, hard journey, were admitted through the massive gate in the city wall, with their precious loads of obsidian, gold or turquoise. Slaves unloaded stone from a sailing ship in the harbour and carried it up to where a new palace was being built, while craftsmen walked down to the quayside for the water they needed to wet their clay or mix their paint or plaster. Ur was already thousands of years old by this time, but it still represented an utterly new phenomenon: urban living.

Ur was among the world's first cities – a conurbation housing thousands of people in a compact area, sustained by food from farmers in the surrounding countryside. Society in Ur was controlled by the priests and kings and queens, whose relative power waxed and waned as they strove for supremacy over each other, over their populace, and over the aggressive enemies who periodically threatened the city. Gradually they perfected the sophisticated techniques of social control that would become essential tools of all future city-builders.

Ur was just one of the great urban centres of Mesopotamia, and its close neighbours – Sumerian cities such as Uruk, Nippur and Kish – were also splendid and majestic at the height of their powers.

CITY CENTRE **Originally there was another platform above the ziggurat at Ur, in Iraq, surmounted by a tower. The massive construction, now so stark, was once planted with trees and decorated with colourful mosaics.**

Each was a city-state, controlling an area of land whose rich agricultural produce not only fed the metropolis but also generated a surplus that allowed a lifestyle of extraordinary luxury for the powerful elite. Although each city was dedicated to a different god, they probably belonged to the same religious tradition, so that the inhabitants of one city would have respected the deity of another. The great city-states bickered over land, water and the control of trade routes, but in times of need they might form alliances against enemies, such as the barbarian hordes from the mountains beyond Mesopotamia, who would swoop down onto the plains, ransacking and looting the cities.

THE ORIGINS OF CITIES

When Ur was at its most powerful, 4000 years ago, it already had a tradition of human occupation. To the populace of its heyday, whether aristocrats or farmers and artisans, it must have seemed as if the city's beginnings were lost in the mists of time. Modern excavations suggest that it originated as a small farming settlement in the riverside plains of what is now southern Iraq about 6500 years ago.

VICTORY FEAST In a panel decorating a lyre, made about 4600 years ago, a Sumerian ruler on his throne is waited on by attendants, and entertained by a musician and a singer; animals and fish are prepared for the banquet.

Extensive excavations at nearby Eridu – which the early inhabitants of Mesopotamia believed to be the oldest of their cities – have shown that the first inhabitants built a simple chapel on the sand dunes, around which were a cluster of small dwellings. The chapel was later dismantled and rebuilt on the same spot, but on a grander scale. Over the ensuing centuries, the religious centre of Eridu was demolished and rebuilt no less than 18

times, culminating in a large and glorious temple. Repeated building on the same holy ground indicates how powerful religious feeling was among the Sumerians and how it endured in much the same form over several millennia.

RELIGION AND RULERS

This strong and stable religious tendency undoubtedly became a major force in the development of urban life – the evidence left in the archaeological record suggests that this heartfelt spirituality was gradually manipulated and transformed, by those seeking power, into an elaborate means of social control and coercion. The pivotal role which religion eventually acquired is apparent at Ur, where the temple demanded substantial offerings of grain, oxen and other produce – particularly butter, oil and gold. This is revealed by detailed accounts, the earliest written records in the world, dating from about 5500 years ago. From these food offerings, meals were cooked for the god twice a day,

THE WORLD ON WHEELS

The wheel was invented in Mesopotamia, and was probably used for making pottery before anyone realised that it could revolutionise the transport of people and goods. From there, it spread to other urbanised areas of the Old World, and to non-urban societies as well. In the New World, the wheel was never put to any practical use, but was incorporated into children's toys.

125

but most food received did not go to the deity. It was stored in the temple complex, instead, and distributed to craftsmen, slaves, the royal family, priests, scribes and aristocrats. No doubt the priests claimed most of the credit for the rich harvest of the land, and stressed their own importance in ensuring that seed sown by the farmers came to life in the soil, that the plants grew, the sun ripened the grain, and the rivers continued to pour their precious waters onto the land. No doubt the people came to believe that, without the intervention of priests and the regular offerings to the temple, food could not be produced.

But a powerful religious faith cannot, in itself, account for the rise of cities and their hierarchical societies – after all, a clever alliance of religion and political power probably controlled most prehistoric societies, as evidenced by the shamans who ministered to the hunters of Ice Age Europe and occasionally figured in their cave paintings. The

BEARERS OF GIFTS   Men bring offerings to a goddess at the Temple of Nin-Gal, next to the ziggurat at Ur. Clay tablets found within the sacred enclosure are inscribed with receipts for goods such as butter and oil.

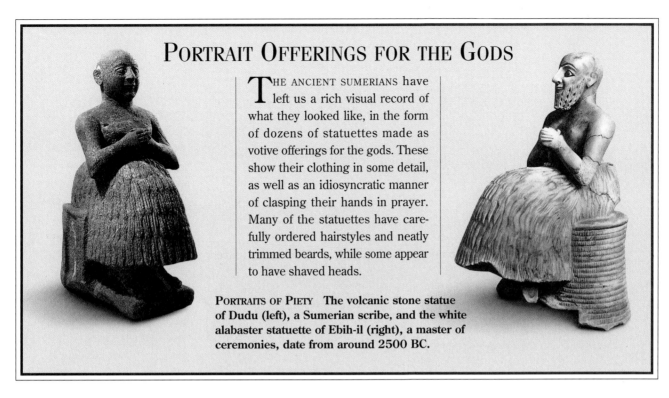

PORTRAIT OFFERINGS FOR THE GODS

THE ANCIENT SUMERIANS have left us a rich visual record of what they looked like, in the form of dozens of statuettes made as votive offerings for the gods. These show their clothing in some detail, as well as an idiosyncratic manner of clasping their hands in prayer. Many of the statuettes have carefully ordered hairstyles and neatly trimmed beards, while some appear to have shaved heads.

PORTRAITS OF PIETY The volcanic stone statue of Dudu (left), a Sumerian scribe, and the white alabaster statuette of Ebih-il (right), a master of ceremonies, date from around 2500 BC.

findings of anthropologists among tribal societies of the 20th century reveal that religion of some kind, whether a belief in gods or simply in unseen spirits, can play a role in structuring such societies today, persuading people to behave in particular ways that suit the society at large.

We can assume that a similar situation may have occurred in prehistory, given the many signs of religious fervour seen in paintings, ceremonial pots, carvings and other artefacts. Yet the majority of prehistoric people did not develop urban living nor the type of society associated with cities, where class divisions were striking and a huge gulf developed between the lifestyle of those in power and that of the common labourers, whether slaves or freemen. By comparing the ancient societies that did urbanise spontaneously with those that did not, archaeologists have hoped to identify certain common factors. Although they have found no single characteristic shared by all of them, the comparisons are still interesting.

AGRICULTURE AND TRADE

Looking only at the Old World, the similarities seem impressive. The four areas of the Old World where complex, stratified urban societies arose – Mesopotamia, Egypt, the Indus Valley and the Huang He (Yellow River) of the Far East – were all located in the flat flood plains of giant meandering rivers, where the soil was alluvial silt brought down

by the waters over the millennia, and extremely fertile as a result. In Egypt, the River Nile irrigated the surrounding land with its annual flood, and the same was probably true in the Indus Valley, but in Mesopotamia and along the Huang He, irrigation was needed to carry the life-giving waters of the rivers to the arid plains where little rain fell. Like the ancient Sumerians, the rulers of Shang Dynasty China diverted the waters of the Huang He onto the farmlands of their kingdom.

In the rich soil of these river valleys, farming was easier than anywhere else on Earth – provided there was water. The fertility of the soil was astonishing, and the abundant harvests of the earliest farmers in these regions may have led to a steady increase in the human population. Over the centuries, more and more people came to be living in these productive valleys. But the abundance of food was offset by a shortage of other natural resources –

SOLID WHEELS A four-wheeled chariot is pulled by asses, from a Sumerian depiction of 4600 years ago.

127

ECHO OF THE PAST In a scene almost unchanged from prehistoric times, this reed-laden boat on the Tigris is moored beside a hut, also made with reeds.

encouraged the emergence of skilled full-time craft-workers, people who did not have to grow their own food but who were fed by the community and allowed to devote themselves exclusively to their craft, producing objects of increasing sophistication and artistry. Given the religious focus of society, these craft-workers would have spent much of their time making figures of the gods or other objects of spiritual significance, and because their increasing skills made the temple yet more breathtaking, they helped to increase the status of their religion further.

Yet more factors came into play where irrigation works were crucial in boosting crop production, as in Mesopotamia and Shang Dynasty China. The irrigation canals of Mesopotamia were probably excavated under the direction of the temple priests and engineers, and the flow of water controlled by religious edict. Farmers would have become yet more dependent on the state for their survival – it was no longer a matter of religious faith alone, for farmers were by now truly dependent on the religious authorities.

Looking at the four great centres of urbanisation in the Old World, it might seem as if a common pattern emerges. But there is a curious flaw. For three of these centres, a crucial factor in the birth of cities was the development of organised religion, enacted in impressive public buildings. But there is no sign of anything comparable in the fourth. The cities of the Indus Valley had temples visible for

broad flood plains such as these, whose trees had been clear-felled long before by the very earliest farmers, lacked timber and stones large enough for building. Mesopotamia did not have sufficient local stone to make items such as sickles. Trade with other areas was the answer, and the surplus food was exchanged for essential raw materials.

Traders were experienced at getting the most from their arduous journeys, even in these prehistoric times, and they liked to tempt their customers with whatever pretty or curious objects they came across in distant lands. For the early farmers of the flood plains, long-distance trade in necessities such as flint and obsidian probably led to trade in luxury goods and exotic items such as gold, copper and precious stones.

It may have been the availability of such decorative raw materials, combined with the abundant food supply, which

SUMERIAN GOLD The holes in this helmet, made from a single sheet of gold alloy, allowed a padded lining to be held in place by laces.

CRAFT AND ARTISTRY Excavated at the royal cemetery at Ur, this 4500-year-old statuette of a goat caught in a thicket is made from gold, silver, shell and red limestone, with lapis lazuli for the blue horns and hair.

miles around, like those of Mesopotamia, while the Egyptians built colossal pyramids for their royal dead who were also deities.

THE GREAT FLOOD

In the early historical records of the Sumerians, one event is of major significance: a huge and devastating flood. Physical signs of the damage done can be found in the lower levels at Ur and other cities. It may have been the same flood as described in the Bible, a much later document.

Yet nothing like this seems to have occurred in the early cities along the Huang He. There are no temples or other places of worship – only palaces and royal tombs. Tracing later Chinese culture back into prehistory, archaeologists have suggested that Chinese religion during the Shang Dynasty focused on ancestor-worship within small family shrines, as it did in later times. Somehow the first emperors managed to establish their hold over the great mass of the people without using the power of grandiose temples and a showy public religion.

Religion did play a huge role in the evolution of urban life in the New World, but in other respects the first cities of Central and South America were substantially different from those of the Old World. Indeed, the one striking similarity seen in the most ancient cities of the Old World – their location in broad river valleys (such as the Indus Valley) – does not occur at all in the Americas. In terms of terrain and agricultural possibilities, the cities of the New World were entirely different from those of Europe and Asia.

What could be more different from the fertile plains of Mesopotamia than the precipitous slopes of the Andes or the bleak deserts of the Peruvian coast, rainless but enveloped by a clammy sea-fog for much of the time? Curiously, it was in this

unpromising landscape that a state-run society arose – the only area of South America to produce such a phenomenon. It began about 3200 years ago, with the Chavín culture, whose most important site was a large temple complex, Chavín de Huantar, built on a massive stone platform.

The similarities with giant platforms constructed in Mesopotamia and other Old World cities is striking. The desire to impress worshippers and subjects was obviously a universal one. Within the platform at Chavín de Huantar there was a maze of

CITYSCAPE **The foundations of Mohenjo Daro, in the Indus Valley, were a triumph of town planning.**

SACRED SITE The ceremonial centre of the Chavín culture, Chavín de Huantar is in the highlands of Peru.

A Son of the Maya King

HE WORE sturdy earrings of polished green jade, and a necklace of jade pendants each showing the figure of a nobleman, or the image of an owl which symbolised death.

Born to the King of the Maya, Smoke Imix, he enjoyed high social standing, but as a younger son he could never hope for power. He was trained as a scribe, a prestigious occupation in a society for whom literacy was something of a novelty and a rare accomplishment.

When he died, in his mid 30s, he was buried in splendour, in a giant tomb cut into a stepped pyramid and lined with massive stone slabs. At the funeral ceremony, incense was burned, and clay effigy figures were dedicated to the dead prince.

The clay cups, which he used to hold ink, and a book made of bark paper were buried with him. So too was a boy, obviously a commoner for his teeth showed signs of arrested growth – evidence that he had experienced hunger. He may have been the personal servant of the prince, sacrificed to accompany his master into the afterlife.

passageways and secret rooms containing images of the gods and other sacred objects. One stood almost 15 ft (4.6 m) high, carved from stone to depict a supreme deity.

This and the other gods of the Chavín culture became part of the traditional religion of the Andes, surviving the demise of one empire to be worshipped again in the next. By about 2200 years ago, the Chavín sphere of influence, which had spanned more than 930 miles (1500 km) off the coast of what is now Peru, went into a decline, but in time it was replaced by two smaller states: the Moche in the north, and the Nazca in the south. The Nazca culture made its own distinctive innovation with the huge depictions of animals on the desert ground, and the Moche people made brilliant advances in ceramics, producing pots that were of unusual excellence even by the high standards of South America. Even so, they were still worshipping the same basic gods inherited from the Chavín culture. These religious traditions continued right through to the much later Inca Empire, which fell to the Spanish conquistadores in the 1530s.

Cities and hierarchical societies arose in Central America at roughly the same time as in South America, and they gathered momentum quickly.

MACABRE ARTISTRY
Colourful feathers and gold discs form the headdress of this Nazca skull, an important ritual object.

They built massive temples on high earth or stone platforms at some sites, impressive stepped pyramids at others, as well as palaces and well-planned populous cities. There were several different cultures, including the Olmec, Zapotec, Maya and later the Aztec. Although each was distinctive, they showed signs of having influenced one another – probably through trade – with similarities in religion and art form. Their gods included a terrifying half-human, half-jaguar figure, snakes, eagles and other animals. Warfare was common, and so was human sacrifice to the gods. One curious feature of these Central American cultures was a sacred ball-game, part sport, part solemn ritual, which took place in specially constructed ball courts. Remains of these walled courts have been found in many of the ancient cities of Central America. In some societies, the losers were sacrificed at the end of the game.

For most people caught up in these revolutionary changes in society, everyday life probably deteriorated rather than improved. Life became vulnerable, as evidenced by the maidservants and retainers put to death and buried in royal tombs with a dead monarch (although the victims themselves might have considered this a great honour). In the tomb of Queen

SITE OF RITUAL SPORT A stone hoop projects from a wall at a ball-game court in Chichén Itzá, Mexico.

Shub-Ad of Ur, 19 men and women were buried along with the corpse of the queen. Evidence suggests that they drank poison before the burial. A grave at Ur contained over 70 slaughtered attendants, while a royal tomb from Shang China held 165 sacrificial victims.

The living were just as subject to royal or priestly wishes. They laboured hard on the construction of temples, platforms, pyramids and palaces, often carrying colossal loads of stone or earth. Compared to the villagers of earlier times, these builders of 'civilisation' must have worked much longer hours, and were probably pushed to the limits of human endurance.

Some were 'free men' who were obliged to pay a labour tax to the state, but many were slaves. Slavery seems to have played a part in at least three of the four Old World centres of urbanisation – Mesopotamia, China and Egypt. It may have originated with a more merciful and mercenary attitude to prisoners of war who, instead of being executed, were put to work rebuilding temples or other public buildings.

Their labour would have increased the power and prestige of the society, and so allowed yet more leisure and luxury for the priests and others in power. As time passed, the rewards of high office became ever greater in these centralised

EARLY WRITING
An 'oracle' bone from Shang Dynasty China. The incised marks can be related, through a series of intermediate forms, with modern Chinese symbols.

and affluent societies, which fuelled social ambition. The thirst for power, luxury and beautiful possessions was undoubtedly a major driving force in the continuing development and elaboration of the great urban societies. Gilded statues, ornate carvings and exquisite jewellery were an intrinsic part of the religious feeling that fuelled them. Beautiful objects inspired devotion, and to be acquisitive, whether for oneself or the temple or society at large, was a mark of piety not greed.

THE END OF PREHISTORY
Prehistory ends when the first written records of a society are made – when history begins. A number of early urbanised societies created their own systems of writing and were therefore responsible for their own transition into history. For most societies, however, history arrived abruptly, often on horse with sword or gun – their first records written by their conquerors. For a few, it arrived in a Land-Rover or light aircraft, as in the highlands of New Guinea, where some isolated villages were only contacted in the 1930s.

Recording history was not a prime motivation for those who first invented writing about 5500 years ago. The earliest literate people were not

STORY IN STONE This stone tablet or implement, engraved with pictograms and an offering scene, was made 5000 years ago in Uruk, a Mesopotamian city.

philosophers, poets or historians – they were accountants. Writing evolved from a system of tokens used in Mesopotamia for making a note of transactions and debts. The tokens were formed from clay, in neat little shapes with incised marks or punched holes added. The shape and markings of a token signified particular goods, such as a cow, dog or sheep, a pottery vessel, stone vessel, bracelet or loaf of bread. To record a payment or a debt, the appropriate tokens would be sealed into a bulla – a hollow bladder-like vessel, also made of clay. As time went by and the system became more refined, marks were made on the outside of the bulla to show what tokens were inside. From there, it was only a short step to making the same marks on a flat piece of clay, and dispensing with the tokens altogether.

PAST TIME A stone 'chessboard' and pieces from Mohenjo Daro, now in Pakistan, are all that remain of a game whose rules have long been forgotten.

This revolutionary invention occurred in the temple precincts of some Mesopotamian city, possibly Uruk, as this is where the oldest incised clay tablets have been found. The amounts of farm produce owed in taxes to the temple were recorded on these tablets, which scribes then stored in special wooden racks. Writing became central to the priestly bureaucracy which governed the Mesopotamian city-states, and for a thousand years this was the only use to which it was put. Only about 2500 years ago was writing used to record the names of kings and their victories in battle – the very first written histories.

Writing also emerged in the urbanised societies of ancient Egypt, Shang Dynasty China, and the Indus Valley at about this time. The Egyptians were probably influenced by Mesopotamia, although it was the concept of writing that they borrowed, rather than the details, and they invented most of their own symbols, as well as their own writing materials – ink and papyrus, rather than damp clay.

The people of China and the Indus Valley invented writing independently of the other regions. The Indus script was only used for short inscriptions on monuments and seals. It has never been deciphered. The first Chinese characters, which are understood, were used for a very singular purpose, the recording of prophecies on the bones of animals, known as oracle bones. The tip of a hot metal rod was applied to each bone, causing it to crack. The pattern made by the cracks was studied by a soothsayer, whose predictions were noted on the bone.

The Maya of Central America produced a system of writing as sophisticated as anything in the Old World. Their intricate and complicated symbols were largely devoted to setting down astronomical observations and astrological predictions, although there are also historical records. Writing was used by other Central American cultures, including the Zapotec. In South America, large and complex empires, including the Incas, survived well without any system of written notation. Debts and other numerical records were made on string with knots.

The varied uses to which writing was put in the early years of its invention, and the fact that some complex large-scale societies got on perfectly well without it, suggest that human inventiveness was, to some extent running ahead of human need. The sudden elaboration of society had led to an explosion of creativity which threw up inventions that were in search of a useful application.

IN A TEMPLE COURTYARD

THE TEMPLE COURTYARD lay at the heart of the Mesopotamian city and was always the scene of intense activity. Children were trained here as scribes, so that one day they would be able to keep records of the produce delivered to the temple; musicians played the harp; and goods, including fish, sheep, fruit and pottery, were traded. Cows were milked, and the milk was then churned and strained to separate the buttermilk from the butterfat. Wrestlers with pots on their heads engaged in ritual contests, which may have portrayed the conflict between semidivine beings such as Gilgamesh and Enkidu. The winner was the one who could lift the other off the ground.

THE PREHISTORIC SOUL

What prompted our ancestors to paint the walls of caves with a magnificent array

of animals or to build massive stone monuments? Anthropologists are now

helping the archaeologists to identify the religious impulses behind prehistoric art.

IN 1879, an amateur archaeologist, Don Marcelino de Sautuola, was exploring a limestone cave he had discovered on his estate at Altamira in northern Spain. The ceilings were very low in the long twisting caverns that snaked through the lime-stone, and Don Marcelino was forced to crawl on his hands and knees but Maria, his four-year-old daughter, was with him and she could stand upright.

It was Maria who noticed the bison on a ceiling in a side chamber. They had been magnificently painted in glowing red ochre and sooty black lines, with the bumps and contours of the cave skilfully used to lend a three-dimensional quality to their muscular haunches and massive humped backs.

The bellowing and charging animals, imbued with a lifelike quality by the long-forgotten artist, were painted with energy, inspiration and extra-ordinary skill. It was an even more remarkable achievement given that the artist was working underground, by the uncertain light of flickering tallow lamps, with difficult materials, and some distance from the living subject-matter. Despite such handicaps, both the essence and the details of the animals were vividly captured.

Why did the hunters of northern Spain, people who lived during the last ice age, about 14 000 years ago, crawl into these caves and paint such works of art? Although more than 200 decorated caves and rock shelters have been discovered in northern Spain and southern France, archaeologists are still answering this crucial question. Cave art flourished at this time and in this particular area, among the hunters of large animals which roamed the landscape. Clearly there was an abundant supply of food in this era. But an abundance of food only explains how people could have afforded to lavish time on artistic endeavours – it does not explain why. Exactly what motivated them?

THE PAINTED BODY: A VANISHING ART

SIGN OF STATUS The tattoo on the right arm of a prehistoric Scythian chieftain is believed to denote his rank.

THE ARTISTRY of many societies finds its greatest expression in the decoration of the human body itself, when skin may be painted or tattooed, scarred in tribal patterns, or raised into bead-like bumps with minute injections of plant juices. Hair may be plaited, tied in knots, dyed, shaved into traditional designs, or stiffened with wax or mud, so that it can be sculpted and arranged. Ears, lips and noses can be pierced, or enlarged into strange and unnatural shapes. This particular form of art may have been common in prehistory but, for the most part, it would have perished with the people themselves. Occasionally there is evidence of such art, for example in the elaborate tattoos found on the skin of Scythian chieftains buried in Siberia and preserved by a mummification process.

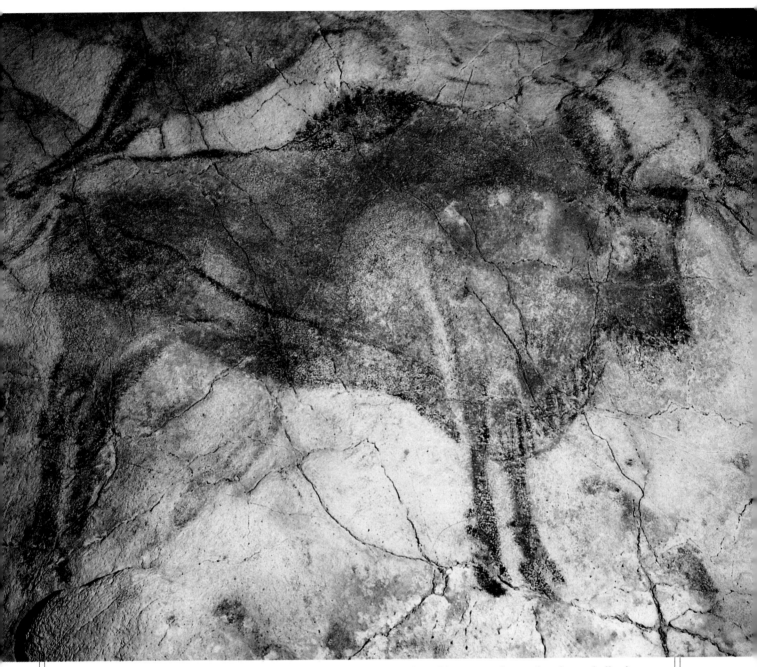

ALTAMIRA ARTISTRY A bison stands his ground; others in the Altamira tableaux are shown charging or bellowing.

The information gathered by anthropologists is extremely helpful when looking at the art of prehistoric people. Anthropologists often work among people who still live in traditional small-scale tribal societies, which have survived into the 20th century relatively untouched by Western customs or other outside influences. Although it is wrong to assume that such people are living replicas of prehistoric societies, they do give some guidelines for interpreting the evidence found by archaeologists.

One consistent discovery made by anthropologists is that the art of tribal societies is intimately connected with their spiritual beliefs and religious practices. The figures shown in paintings or incised into a pottery bowl are likely to be those of gods, demons or ancestors. Animals carved on a wooden paddle or etched onto the bone handle of a knife will be totemic or sacred creatures, and even the shape of the paddle or knife may symbolise some ancient belief. The colour and style of headdresses and the design of face-paint patterns will in some way illustrate tribal myths, such as creation stories or tales about the tribe's origin. In such a society, every single image reinforces communal beliefs.

Art, religion, customs, family relationships and tribal law are usually interwoven so tightly that they create a social fabric, resilient and strong enough to hold people together through all kinds of conflict and adversity. The close relationship of religion with art and social customs creates an all-embracing culture, where every man-made object

BODY PAINT Kwakiutl boys, from the north-west coast of North America, are painted as bears for a ritual dance.

encountered by day, every legend retold, even the most mundane greeting or proverb, reinforces traditional values and encourages people to live by the accepted codes.

It is reasonable to assume that in prehistoric times art did have a depth of meaning, and that far from being purely decorative or practised just for amusement, artistic activities were loaded with

spiritual significance. 'Art for art's sake' seems to be a peculiarly modern notion.

When a particular artistic tradition endured for centuries or even millennia, as it did in southern France and northern Spain during the last phase of the ice ages, we can guess that there was also a relatively stable social structure which accompanied it. The recurring themes and styles seen in the paintings of Altamira, the famous caves of Lascaux in southern France, and other caves in the region, point to a durable culture which was passed on from generation to generation over thousands of years. This in turn suggests that, even in prehistoric times, people lived through the same marriage of religion and politics that anthropologists find among tribal people today.

In a few parts of the world, there appears to be a continuous tradition between the art of prehistoric times and that of the present day. On the Jos

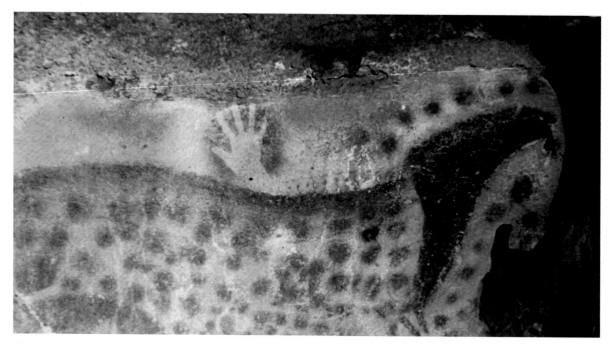

SPOTS AND SIGNS The front of a horse, from Lascaux, is depicted with spots on its body and neck. Hand-prints were made by using the hand as a stencil and then blowing paint at the area through a hollow plant stem.

THE POWERFUL SHAMAN

Found in some of the painted caves of southern France are depictions of strange figures that are half-human, half-animal. Menacing individuals, they seem to be dancing or engaged in a ritual activity.

These have been interpreted as shaman figures, or 'witchdoctors', known from surviving tribal societies. In such societies, the shamans have supernatural powers and are responsible for remembering the ancient wisdom of their tribe. They are possessors

of magic spells, and healers of both body and spirit – which is why they are sometimes also known as 'medicine-men'.

The shadowy figures in the cave paintings suggest that the shamans played an important part in the animal-centred religion of Ice Age Europe.

STRANGE CREATURE
This shaman figure, part human, part stag, was painted on the wall of a cave in France about 13 000 years ago.

plateau of Nigeria, about 2300 years ago, sculptors were modelling human heads from clay – superbly stylised heads of extraordinary vigour. These people are known to archaeologists as part of the Nok culture. This developed into the later Yoruba culture, which continued to produce terracotta heads and also developed a tradition of casting heads in bronze. Some of the bronzes produced in Ife, the ancient capital of a Yoruba kingdom, rank among the most stunning works of art produced by prehistoric peoples. The artistic traditions of the Yoruba culture continue to this day.

BEYOND HUNTING MAGIC

Given that the cave paintings of the ice age may have spiritual significance, can we work out what role they played in people's lives? One of the early suggestions pointed to hunting magic – painting an animal in order to secure it in the next day's hunt. The fact that the images are usually painted on top of one another, or overlapping in incongruous ways, suggests that the individual animals were what mattered to these artists, rather than the overall composition. Altamira cave is unusual in that the images are part of a well-composed picture that includes several animals. The magnificent Lascaux paintings share this distinction with Altamira,

but in most caves the paintings are a chaotic jumble of individual images.

The problem with the hunting-magic explanation is that the animal most commonly used for food, the reindeer, whose bones are found in abundance wherever the hunters lived, scarcely ever features in the paintings. Moreover, the artists usually worked in uninhabited caves, and often painted in particularly awkward and inaccessible sites within those caves. This implies that their work had some special mystic significance, far removed from everyday hunting and survival. It seems that the caves where they were painted were sacred sites.

As well as the animals, there are often geometric patterns, rows of dots, indecipherable symbols and hand-prints made by blowing paint from a hollow straw against a hand held up on the cave wall. These may just be prehistoric doodles, but it is much more likely that the ice age hunters were already capable of symbolism and abstract thought.

THE BIRTH AND DEATH OF CULTURES

With the end of the ice age and the disappearance of large game, the great artistic tradition that produced Lascaux and Altamira died out. But at other times and in other places, the human spirit once again produced an explosion of artistic creation and cultural innovation. These new cultures each arose gradually, became more and more elaborate over the centuries, then finally died out.

Why did such flourishing traditions eventually wither? This may be answered by looking at an artistic tradition that spans the gap between prehistory and modern times. In southern Africa 2000 years ago, a tradition of rock painting developed which produced magnificent portrayals of game animals and human hunters. This tradition survived, with gradual changes in painting styles and subject-matter, into historical times – rock paintings were still being produced by the !Kung San, or Bushmen, of the Kalahari Desert in the early years of the 20th century. Only now has the ancient tradition died out, following the steady erosion of the !Kung San way of life – a belated consequence of European settlement in South Africa. It seems likely that the disappearance of many of the cultures that flourished during prehistory can be explained in much the same way: conquest or colonisation.

The Dawn of Religion

Thousands of years before the first paintings or carvings were made, prehistoric people had begun to bury their dead. This practice, which probably began about 100 000 years ago, was first adopted by the Neanderthal people living in Europe and south-west Asia. Not everyone was buried, and many Neanderthals were simply left where they had fallen, but others were buried with ceremony and special offerings. At Teshik Tash in Central Asia in what is now Uzbekistan, close to the Afghan border, a Neanderthal boy was buried in a cave. Around his body the mourners placed large horns from mountain goats. Nearby a fire was lit, perhaps to keep people warm during the ceremony, or to roast the meat of the goats which may have been eaten as a funeral feast.

At Shanidar cave in what is now Iraq several Neanderthal people were buried 50 000 years ago. Careful microscopic examination of the sediment shows high concentrations of pollen, suggesting that flowers were laid around the corpse as it was buried. This may simply have been a mark of affection, as funeral flowers are today, or the plants could have been medicinal herbs. More commonly found in prehistoric burials was the pigment red ochre, also widely used in rituals and rock paintings, and possibly symbolic of life and warmth.

As the millennia passed, burial became more and more common. By the time prehistoric people were living in permanent settlements, either the burial or cremation of the dead was essential to prevent a build-up of corpses and the consequent smell and spread of disease. But there was a great deal more involved than purely practical considerations, as the relentless elaboration of funeral rites shows. At a site called Vounous in northern Cyprus, a cemetery dating from 4000 years ago has been excavated. The earliest burials were made in simple pits, but in time these became larger and eventually the dead were buried in imposing tombs cut from the rock. At the same time, there was a steady increase in the goods buried with the dead which became both

Old Masters !Kung San of the Kalahari in Africa examine rock paintings made by their ancestors. Those made in more recent times continue the artistic tradition.

LAST RITES Some Neanderthal people buried their dead, and may even have placed flowers around the body.

more numerous and more elaborately made. Special pots, with highly decorated surfaces, and shapes that would have been of little practical use, were buried with the dead. It seems likely that these were made solely for this purpose.

A similar elaboration of funeral rites can be seen in the Near East from about 12 000 years ago. In some of the oldest houses, the skulls of the dead have been buried beneath the floor of the dwelling. This meant that they would lie beneath the feet of the living as the inhabitants went about their daily business. To bury the skull in this way, they probably exposed corpses in the open, beyond the town boundary, so that the flesh would be pecked away by vultures and the bones washed clean by the rain. Only then would the whitened skull be taken back to the ancient city of Jericho and buried. As time went by, the treatment given to the skulls of Jericho's revered dead became yet more elaborate. Facial features were re-created on the skulls using white plaster, with cowrie shells inserted for the eyes. The skulls were then buried beneath the house floor. An equally elaborate treatment

DEATH MASK A skull found in Jericho has facial features modelled onto it using clay, and cowrie shells in place of the eyes.

was seen among many other prehistoric people. In the long barrows of Britain – communal tombs constructed about 6000 years ago – the bodies were probably left outside the tomb in an open place to rot before the bones were taken into the long barrow. In some tombs, the bones of each skeleton were separated and grouped with bones from other skeletons, skulls being placed in one area of the long barrow, the long leg bones in another, and so on. Sometimes the bones of men were placed in one chamber, while those of women and children were left in other chambers.

In the desert areas of Peru, people took advantage of the extraordinarily dry climate to turn corpses into mummies. They were bundled up in cloth and left in caves or strapped onto wooden frames to keep the body straight. In some parts of South America, the mummies were brought out during certain religious festivals so that people could see their ancestors – a macabre ritual that was reported by the early Spanish conquistadores. Deliberate mummification of the dead was also practised by the islanders of the Torres Strait, the stretch of sea that lies

between Australia and New Guinea. Having preserved the body of a dead relative, the islanders
then painted the body with red ochre and painted
the head black with a red band on the forehead.
Pieces of shell were then placed in the eye-sockets
to represent eyes.

All these complex rites, as well as the elaborate
ceremonies associated with cremation, suggest a
profound concern with the fate of human beings
after they have died. It was the price humans paid
for their greater intelligence. Unlike their ape-like
forebears, they realised that one day they must die,

and the fear of annihilation fostered a great variety
of rituals surrounding the dead, all centred around
a belief in spiritual survival after death. For many
prehistoric societies, it seems as if the time and
energy devoted to the dead far exceeded the effort
expended on living.

FEAR OF THE DEAD
The idea that human beings survived in some way
beyond death had its comforts, but also its terrors.
It is clear from certain finds that prehistoric people
were often afraid of ghosts and the malevolent

spirits of the dead. Many of the bodies found preserved in peat bogs in northern Denmark were pinned down in the bog by forked sticks, or had branches laid across the body, as if to ensure that they did not rise from their watery graves. One woman drowned in a bog at Haraldskjaer was enclosed in a kind of cage created by birchwood poles stuck vertically into the peat all around the body, with other poles laid horizontally across the top. In Germany, at a site called Kreepen, near Hanover, a woman's body had been secured with rings of iron around the knees and one arm, as well as oak planks and

stones. All these corpses seem to have been of people who were executed for some offence, or in some cases they could have been human sacrifices to the gods.

Veneration of the dead is another, contrasting practice – demonstrated by many prehistoric discoveries. The effort put in to making long barrows

SPIRITUAL STATION The barrow at Newgrange, in Ireland, is 280 ft (85 m) in diameter and 40 ft (12 m) high. It is a huge communal tomb with astronomical alignments.

and some other communal tombs in prehistoric Europe suggests an obsession with ancestors and the past. It seems likely that this focus on the deceased was connected with maintaining social order and established customs. From studies of anthropologists, we know that the fear of retribution by irate ancestors can be a very effective means of perpetuating the existing social structure and shoring up traditions. Priests and shamans do not just give comfort and perform rituals – they are also very powerful figures who claim to speak for the departed ancestors, and who interpret the meaning of illness and other calamities, often blaming the victim for transgressions against taboos, or explaining a misfortune in terms of witchcraft by others. In claiming to speak for the dead and interpret their wishes, these spiritual leaders control and direct people's lives.

DEATH'S RICTUS A 2000-year-old pottery vessel from Mexico features a grinning skull as a representation of death.

low-ceilinged passage which led from the outside world into the main chamber. From there, even narrower passages led off to three smaller chambers where the bodies were actually left. All these passages were built, not at ground level, but raised some way above the floor.

One archaeologist has suggested that the experience of crawling through these passages, which would have been pitch-black and filled with the stench of death, allowed the living to experience death briefly for themselves. Coming through them into the vaulted chamber, lit brightly by oil lamps, would perhaps have reassured the mourners that there was indeed life after death.

The contents of Maes Howe were looted, probably by Norse raiders, more than 1000 years ago and the bodies also disappeared. From surviving remains, it seems likely that this was a communal tomb used by the local rulers for the burial of themselves, their ancestors and their descendants. The great circular mound sticking up from the surrounding landscape would have served to remind the humbler people where their allegiance lay.

In South and Central America, death once again figured prominently in the civilisations of prehistory. Human sacrifice became an entrenched tradition in many of these civilisations, the supply of victims being sustained by warfare and conquest. At the same time, dead ancestors were venerated and festivals of the dead, such as those in Peru where the mummies were paraded, were a central part of the culture. Skulls feature heavily in the art objects of the Aztecs and in several other cultures. Scenes of violence are commonly depicted, and grim faces stare out from pots, mosaics, masks and textiles.

Among the most ancient art objects in the world are small figurines, found at many different sites in Europe, and carved from bone, antler or sometimes

CULTS OF THE DEAD

The tomb of Maes Howe in Orkney, off northern Scotland, is an outstanding example of the effort that Neolithic subsistence farmers of 4700 years ago willingly expended to commemorate the dead. Built of stone with supreme skill, the huge domed chamber of the tomb soars 15 ft (4.6 m) high inside. The whole structure is covered by a circular earth mound, 24 ft (7 m) high and 115 ft (35 m) in diameter.

Getting into the burial chambers with a corpse, or even without one, was no simple matter. First, the mourners had to negotiate a long, narrow,

TWO-FACED A clay head, from Mexico, is believed to represent the duality between life and death.

SPRING WEDDING
This circular stone, from Sweden, was engraved about 2500 years ago, and is thought to symbolise the union of a god and goddess in their sacred spring wedding.

stone. Dating from the ice age, they depict women with enlarged breasts, stomachs and buttocks. They were probably modelled on real, possibly pregnant, women. Despite the basic realism of these figurines, there is also a stylised repetitive quality to them, with their short hair, rotund build, pendulous breasts and downward-looking faces.

FERTILITY RITES

Some experts have half-jokingly suggested that these figurines constituted the earliest pornography, and others that they represented the ideal woman of the times. But most historians agree that they indicate a fertility cult, in which a goddess was worshipped who had powers over the fecundity of both animals and human kind.

The figures date from between about 25 000 years ago and 14 000 years ago, although similar images of women are known from many other parts of the prehistoric world, suggesting that fertility cults were a recurring theme. During the Iron Age in northern Europe, beginning around 1000 years ago, highly stylised fertility goddesses were being cast in iron to be used as amulets. In these figures, breasts and stomach are symbolised by nothing more lifelike than geometric cones or hemispheres.

By contrast, rock carvings from Bohusln in Sweden are explicit, if cartoon-like, in their portrayal of the sacred spring wedding which renews the fertility of the earth. Both male and female figures are shown, probably representing gods and goddesses of fertility enacting the drama of the seasons. These carvings date from the Bronze Age, about 2500 years ago. Other contemporary representations of the fertility goddess show her wearing a

A DAY IN THE LIFE OF

A PREHISTORIC PSYCHOLOGIST FROM THE ARCTIC

THE HUMAN CONDITION   A caribou antler, carved with 27 human faces, is a catalogue of emotions.

BY THE WARMTH OF THE FIRE, with all the important work of the day complete, the man could at last get on with his carving. He took out the piece of caribou antler and his stone knife, and set to work on a new face.

Earlier, a party of hunters had returned from a hazardous trip, and he had noticed the happy, beaming face of a mother greeting her son. He added her to his collection of faces, capturing her expression with skilful strokes of the knife. There were already more than 20 faces on the piece of antler, some angry or sad, others hostile, downcast, crying, laughing, serene or in pain. By the time the carving was complete, there would be 27 different faces crammed together on the antler – which happened to be found 2500 years later, near the place within the Arctic Circle where the prehistoric student of human nature had camped. He belonged to a breed of Arctic people, known to archaeologists as the makers of the 'Dorset Culture', who lived in Alaska and northern Canada before the ancestors of the Eskimos.

STANDING STONES The stone circle at Castlerigg, near Keswick in northern England – photographed at dawn on midsummer's

collar, with her hands held under her breasts as if to nurture the world. On a silver cauldron from Gundestrup in Denmark, a goddess like this is shown travelling on a wagon surrounded by mythical beasts. It is clear that wagons were associated with the goddess and many were placed in bogs as special sacrifices to her. We know about such sacrifices because the acid waters of the bogs have often preserved the wooden wheels and the bodywork of the wagon to this day.

Above the stone slab that blocks the entrance to the Maes Howe grave is a fine slit edged by stones. In midwinter, the shortest day of the year, the setting sun shines directly onto this slit, and its dull red light travels straight down the long, narrow entrance tunnel to penetrate the central chamber of the tomb. On no other day and at no other time can the sun's rays reach the chamber. This might be dismissed as a chance effect unintended by the builders of the tomb, if similar effects were not also

day – is one of many such monuments erected in Britain and north-western France between 5000 and 3500 years ago.

observed time and time again in prehistoric monuments. At the massive stone temple of Newgrange in Ireland, a similar slit exists above the entrance, but here it is the midwinter sunrise that shines in through the slit and whose rapier-like rays pierce the gloom of a long passage to reach the chambers where ancestral bones were worshipped.

Maes Howe dates from about 4700 years ago, Newgrange from 5200 years ago, and there are many other tombs and massive stone constructions from the same era that are aligned to significant positions of the Moon or Sun. A stone circle in Cumbria known as Long Meg and Her Daughters has an entrance-way and outlying standing stone which form a line pointing to the midwinter sunset. At Castlerigg, nearby, there is a sight-line to the midsummer sunset from the tallest stone. At Clava, in Scotland, the cairn is aligned with the extreme southerly point on the horizon where the moon rises, with the points where it sets, and with other points where it would have been at its greatest height in the southern sky 5000 years ago. Stonehenge, the most famous of stone circles, situated on the plateau of Wiltshire in southern England, has sight-lines to points where the Sun rises and sets at both midwinter and midsummer, and other sight-lines to the northernmost points at which the Moon sets during the year and the southernmost points at which it rises.

THE FIRST ASTRONOMERS

The interest of prehistoric people in astronomic events is unquestioned, but why they were interested is still debated. Were they interested in the behaviour of the Sun and Moon in an abstract semiscientific way? Were they hoping to predict seasonal changes in order to improve agricultural performance? Or were these alignments simply a means to some spiritual end? Some archaeologists of today tend to favour the last view, that they had a spiritual end in mind. They draw parallels with beliefs recorded among people such as the Caroline Islanders of the Pacific, who think that when the new moon rises in the sky their dead ancestors come alive again, that the ancestors rejoice and flourish as the Moon waxes, but die once again as it wanes.

MEXICAN SNAKE At certain times of the year, the sun's rays cast 'a serpent of sunshine' on the stairway at Chichén Itzá in Mexico. The snake's head is at the bottom left.

Similarly, the Mantung Indians of Dakota used to expose a dead person on a timber platform with the feet facing the rising Sun to reawaken its soul for eternal life. Navajo Indians also traditionally believe that death is linked with the Sun and Moon. It seems likely that prehistoric people were acting upon such beliefs when they oriented their tombs and monuments towards the most significant positions of the Sun and Moon.

If these beliefs prevailed, rather than simply a scientific interest in astronomy, an astonishing degree of careful observation and patient recording was required to achieve the alignments on midwinter and midsummer positions. To establish sight-lines on the most northerly or most southerly positions of the Moon was an even more staggering task, requiring detailed observations over a period of decades. That such observation was possible suggests the existence of specialists, whose food and clothing were supplied by others so that they could dedicate a great deal of their time to astronomy.

Many other prehistoric cultures also paid great attention to the movements of the Sun, Moon and stars, particularly the Maya of Central America,

SEEING THE FUNNY SIDE OF PREHISTORIC LIFE

OCCASIONALLY, a sense of humour is evident in prehistoric art, as in some of the small carvings that date from the ice age.

One recurring subject is a deer with its head twisted round to look at a bird perched on the deer's own droppings. Something about the deer's pose suggests a jokey quality to the carvings. Despite this, they are executed with great skill and sensitivity, in keeping with many other carved items from this time.

A clay figurine from Nayurit, in western Mexico, dating from about 1000 years ago, shows a man with a huge headdress, or an elaborate hairdo, lying in bed, his head supported by a neck-rest, with the headdress or hairdo – whichever it is – projecting comically from the top of the bed. Perhaps this figurine was a satirical comment on the fashions of the time.

GIANT TRACES ON THE LANDSCAPE

MANY OF THE CONSTRUCTIONS of prehistoric times are utterly mystifying. The strange lines drawn some 2000 years ago on the Nazca desertlands of northern Peru are perhaps the most famous example. Formed by removing stones to leave clearer, paler ground, they depict animals, but on a vast scale, so that the pictures can only be comprehended when seen from an aeroplane. The creators of these gigantic pictures can never have seen what they looked like in their totality, and must have laid out the lines by a careful process of extrapolation from smaller sketches. Presumably the drawings were meant to be seen from the sky, by gods or spirits. Even more puzzling are the long straight ditches, made in parallel pairs, which run for up to 6 miles (10 km) across the English countryside – in Wiltshire, for example. They are known as cursuses, since it was once erroneously believed that they were used for racing horses, but this explanation is now rejected in favour of some kind of ceremonial role. A few of the cursuses seem to have astronomical alignments to the Sun or Moon.

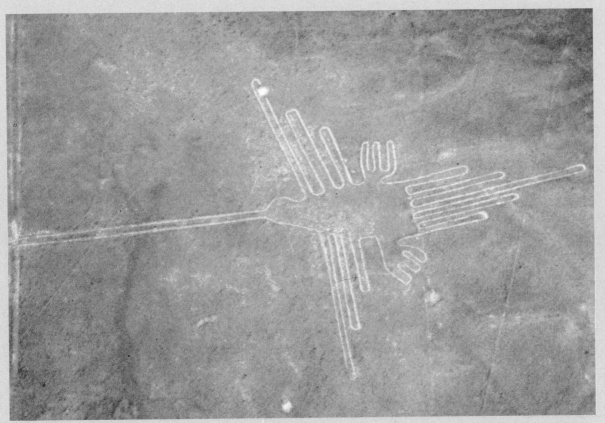

FLIGHTLESS BIRD A remarkable image of a hummingbird sprawls across the desert in the Nazca valley in Peru.

whose temple at Uaxactuan in Guatemala shows complex alignments with the sunrise on the longest day, the sunrise on the shortest day, and the sunrise at the equinoxes. The ability to predict eclipses of the Sun and the Moon, and the path of planets such as Venus, gave the Maya priests a great deal of authority and power over the people.

Religion permeated many prehistoric societies in a way that we would find difficult to comprehend today. Religion was life, and life was religion, so that people directed most of their thought and action toward the fulfilment of spiritual goals, whether it was the elaborate treatment of the dead, the careful observation and worship of the Sun, Moon and other heavenly bodies, or the creation of temples and monuments. The massive stone

ROCKS OF AGES   The present-day stones of Stonehenge, in southern England, are the tattered remnants of a massive unbroke

statues of Easter Island are a case in point. Recent experiments have shown that it was indeed possible for human beings, unaided either by mythical giants or modern machinery, to stand the colossal statues upright on their platforms. It could be done by means of ropes pulling the statues along on sledges and required about 180 people, all pulling simultaneously on the ropes, to move a statue weighing more than 10 tons.

THE SPIRITUAL ENERGY OF STONEHENGE

Once it reached the chosen site, the statue was very gradually levered upright with ropes and wedges, then finally allowed to slip onto the stone platform. Thousands of men must have been

involved in making and erecting the statues, a large sacrifice of manpower for a relatively small island, and there must also have been many accidents that cost countless lives.

Stonehenge is just as much a monument to the patience and spiritual energy of prehistoric humankind. In its original form, it was a circle of 30 upright stones each weighing about 25 tons. These were all linked in an unbroken circle by horizontal lintels laid on top of the uprights and locked into position on them by mortise joints. Close inspection of the site reveals just how much trouble was taken. The upright stones are beautifully shaped, with their surfaces smoothed flat by thousands of hours of persistent labour. The horizontal lintels

...ircle – a major ceremonial centre built by early farmers about 4000 years ago.

each have a gentle curve to them and are fitted together so that they form a perfect circle. The lintels and uprights are locked together by mortise and tenon joints, a technique derived from woodworking but infinitely more difficult to achieve with stone.

Archaeologists have established that the stones were pulled upright by huge wooden levers operated by ropes from below, with timber platforms used to wedge the stone as it rose gradually. In the final stage, the colossal stone was pulled upright by pulling on ropes from the other side. The lintels may have been raised by constructing temporary earth or rubble-stone platforms around the upright stones and then dragging the lintels up to the top. Or they could have been raised on timber platforms that were built around the vertical stones with the horizontal lintels being levered up, little by little, as the platform rose in height. Stonehenge was built about 4000 years ago, towards the end of the Stone Age period in Britain, although it was sited on an earlier cemetery which was enclosed by a circular ditch dug about 4800 years ago. There were dozens of other henges built from stone at about this time, as well as timber henges and stone circles that were much less elaborately made.

Much later, impressive round barrows were constructed for the dead, as well as many other strange and impressive constructions – as these prehistoric people sought to turn the landscape into a huge declaration of their spiritual ideas.

Time Chart

Means of Subsistence

Hunting and gathering – collecting plant foods – sustained all human beings thoughout the world, whether Neanderthals or anatomically modern people. During the ice ages, when the climate and vegetation changed dramatically in the Northern Hemisphere, hunting had to provide the major part of the diet. Large game animals such as mammoths and bison began to fall prey to the more organised and skilful bands of hunters of this era. Most of Africa,

TAKE AIM An ice age hunter of 15 000 years ago uses a spear-thrower for greater speed and thrust.

Europe and Asia was inhabited, except the very coldest regions close to the ice sheets. People had migrated southwards into New Guinea and Australia, but North and South America had probably not yet been colonised. As the ice ages came to an end, migrating herds of animals, moving south through a newly opened ice-free corridor in North America, lured bands of Siberian hunters after them, initiating the settlement of a whole new continent. Within a few thousand years, descendants of these people had reached South America. With the melting of the ice sheets, food

GAME ANIMALS A bison, modelled in clay from Lascaux, France.

resources changed. The large game of the ice ages began to disappear, and people relied more on plant foods and the meat of small animals. Permanent settlements sprang up in food-rich areas, such as coastal zones with abundant shellfish.

Tools and Technology

At the beginning of this period, wood, bone, antler and stone were the main raw materials. Plant fibres may well have been used to make baskets, string and other useful items, but no evidence of these has survived.

In colder regions, clothing was made from animal hides. Around 20 000 years ago, sewn clothing began to be made, using needles crafted from bone or antler. The Neanderthals (who either died out or were assimilated by anatomically modern people during this era) made a distinctive set of stone tools using their own special

ANTLER WEAPONS These harpoons, made from deer's antler, were found at the mesolithic site at Star Carr in Yorkshire, England.

technique. The toolmaking skills of most human groups became more and more sophisticated as the millennia passed.

Stone tools continued to become more finely made. They were generally much smaller so that less

raw material was required. Small sharp blade tools, which were used until blunt and then discarded, became the norm. Dozens of blades might be used up for a task such as skinning an animal.

Spear-throwers were invented and made the business of hunting far easier. The first fishing nets and fish traps made of basketry were probably being produced around 10 000 years ago.

Pottery originated in Japan from about 12 000 years ago, and the first potters of this region quickly achieved some sophisticated pots decorated with linear relief. One of the most important early pottery sites was at Fukui Cave.

Social and Spiritual Life

People lived in small groups and most kept on the move, with no permanent homes. There was little hierarchy in most societies: everyone was more or less equal, although some groups living in the extreme climate of Siberia probably had hereditary chieftains.

Traces of the pigment red ochre from the earliest part of this epoch suggest that spiritual life had already begun in some form, and it was to evolve rapidly over the centuries that

ANCIENT BEAUTY This ivory head was carved by ice age hunters in central Europe.

followed. Burial of the dead, although not universally practised, had become reasonably common around 20 000 years ago. Art had also begun to flourish in some regions of the world, notably Africa and south-west Europe, with rock paintings and small carved objects.

The magnificent cave paintings of Lascaux in south-west France, Altamira in northern Spain, and other sites in south-west Europe were created between 20 000 and 10 000 years ago – a pinnacle of artistic achievement

that reflected a stable, flourishing and creative society.

Shamans or medicine men were powerful figures who probably had both religious and political roles. Burying the dead had become a more common practice by the end of the period, and often there were gifts placed in the grave.

Other evidence suggests that some kind of ritual or funeral feast had taken place for many of the dead. In some societies, the flowering of the human spirit was expressed in the elaboration of tools, some of which were now so exquisitely made that they were far too delicate for practical use, and were more probably purely ornamental or prestige items.

In several parts of the world, people started to settle in one area and grow their own food. Agriculture originated first in the Fertile Crescent of the Middle East, spreading from there into nearby regions. It began independently in the Far East and the Americas. Vast areas remained uncultivated as people continued with the ancient hunter-gatherer lifestyle, although not all of these were nomadic: hunter-gatherer settlements were a feature of many coastal regions, especially in northern Europe, Japan and parts of North America.

About 3500 years ago, people who had settled the islands of the Pacific Ocean began to migrate eastwards and reached Fiji, Tonga and Samoa,

GROWTH RECORD Three stages in the evolution of corn cob (maize), from 7000 to 500 years ago.

bringing with them crops such as breadfruit and yams. In the Americas, agriculture based on maize as the staple crop became well established in Central America and the Andes region. About 3000 years ago, agriculture was introduced into the south-west of North America, and gradually spread to the rest of the continent.

In the last 2000 years, agriculture continued to spread to new regions, particularly in North America, where more and more northerly groups of hunter-gatherers adopted the cultivation of maize, beans and squash. In the Pacific region, farming people reached Hawaii, bringing traditional crops and domesticated animals. Other colonisers sailed onwards to Easter Island, and a few boats may have reached the South American mainland. In New Zealand, yam, taro and sweet potato were grown in the warmer coastal areas of North Island but most of South Island was too cold for the cultivation of these crops, and it therefore had a population of hunters and gatherers.

MEANS OF SUBSISTENCE

METAL CASTING This statuette of a two-wheeled chariot was cast from copper about 4700 years ago.

Between about 10 000 and 5000 years ago, there was a fashion for tiny stone tools, called microliths; the bow and arrow were invented for hunting small game; and pottery

making spread to many new areas, and was independently invented in the Americas. For farming people with food to store, it became an essential item. Farmers also needed a variety of novel stone tools such as sickles, querns to grind cereals, and axes to chop trees.

From about 5000 years ago, the smelting of ores was applied to the making of bronze and later of iron for weapons and prestige items. In time, the value of metal axes became evident. In the heavily wooded regions of northern Europe, and later in Central Africa,

metal axes greatly speeded the clearance of forest for agriculture. Stone, wood and bone continued to be essential raw materials for many different tools. The wheel was invented in Mesopotamia, first for use in making pottery, and only later for transport. From about 2000 years ago, trade was flourishing between regions that were still living in prehistory, and others that had invented writing and had thus become part of 'history'.

EARLY RECORD This clay tablet from Mesopotamia deals with field ownership.

TOOLS AND TECHNOLOGY

Images of gods begin to appear from about 10 000 years ago, such as at Lepenski Vir, a village on the Danube river where each of the wooden huts had a stone fish-god figure set beside the hearth. Bull worship was practised at the farming settlement of Çatal Hüyük in the Near East, while at Jericho people worshipped their dead ancestors. Signs of increasing tension between different groups of people appear at this time, as in the heavy fortifications at Jericho.

The first cities and hierarchical societies developed in Mesopotamia, dependent on taxes paid by farmers in the surrounding countryside. Writing was invented, although only used for accounting at first. The idea

of city-states and priestly bureaucracies probably spread from Mesopotamia to Egypt. Similar developments took place in China and the Indus Valley of northern India. At a later date, stratified societies based on an organised religion developed independently in Central and South America.

In the areas that remained prehistoric, social and spiritual life often developed a unique regional character. Huge monuments such as Stonehenge were built in northern Europe nearly 2000 years ago. Complex societies could still develop, as at the massive stone-built city of Great Zimbabwe in Africa.

Contact with literate societies continued to influence prehistoric cultures.

BURIAL CHAMBER Stones in a passage grave in northern France are carved in a style common in Britain and Ireland.

SOCIAL AND SPIRITUAL LIFE

INDEX

ACKNOWLEDGMENTS

Abbreviations:
T=Top; M=Middle; B=Bottom; R=Right; L=Left

AAAC=The Ancient Art & Architecture Collection
AKG=Archiv für Kunst und Geschichte, London
TBA=Toucan Books Archive, London

1 Musée de l'Homme, Collection Henri Lhote/AKG; 2-3 Photograph Mark Oliver; 4 Photograph B. & C. Alexander, TL; Peter Kain © Richard Leakey, TR. 5 Römisch-Germanisches Zentralmuseum, TL; Photograph Michael Holford, TR; Thomas F. Lynch, Brazos Valley Museum, ML; Photograph Ira Block, BM; Devizes Museum, Wiltshire, BR. 6-7 Illustration by Sarah Kensington. 7 Science Photo Library, TL. 9 Science Photo Library. 10 Science Photo Library. 11 Illustration by Sarah Kensington. 12 Illustration by David Noonan. 13 Science Photo Library. 15 NHPA/ Martin Harvey. 16 Illustration by David Noonan. 17 Map by Nick Skelton. 18 Illustration by David Noonan. 19 Hutchison Library/J. Wright. 20-21 Tappeiner. 22 Illustration by Paul Wright. 23 Frank Spooner Pictures/Gamma/ Paul Hanny; TM. Römisch-Germanisches Zentralmuseum/ Christin Beeck, MM; Römisch-Germanisches Zentralmuseum, BM. 24-25 Illustration by Jim Russell. 26-27 Hutchison Library/Jesco von Puttkamer. 28 Illustration by David Noonan. 29 AKG/Walter Grunwald. 30 Illustration by Paul Wright. 31 Illustration by David Noonan, TM; illustration by Sarah Kensington, TR; Römisch-Germanisches Zentralmuseum, B. 32 Novosti Photo Library. 33 National Museum, Copenhagen/AKG/Eric Lessing. 34 Illustration by David Noonan. 35 AKG/Eric Lessing. 36 Archäologisches Landesmuseum, TL, BL; illustration by Sarah Kensington, TR; National Museum, Copenhagen, BR. 37 Biofotos/Heather Angel, T; National Museum, Copenhagen, BL, BM, BR. 38 Natural History Museum,

Vienna/AKG/Eric Lessing, BL. 38-39 Illustration by Paul Wright. 40 Thomas F. Lynch, Brazos Valley Museum. 41 Illustration by David Noonan. 42 Illustration by Sarah Kensington, TL; Musée Municipal D'Archéologie, Lons-Le-Saunier/Photograph H. Masure, BM. 43 The Cleveland Museum of Art, The Norweb Collection. 44 Peruvian Textile, from Documents d'Art: Art Ornemental des Tissus Indiens du Vieux Pérou by R. and M. Harcourt, Editions Albert Morance, 1924, TL; Photograph John Bigelow Taylor, B. 45 Illustration by David Noonan, TL; Mummy Bundle, Paracas, from Paracas, Primera Parte by Julio C. Tello, Empressa Gráfica T. Scheuch S.A., 1959, TR. 46-47 Robert Harding Picture Library/R. Clevenger. 48 Map by Nick Skelton. 49 Robert Estall/Alastair Scott. 50 Photograph Warren Morgan. 51, 52 Maps by Nick Skelton. 53 Prof R.C. Green, Department of Anthropology, University of Auckland. 54 MSI. 55 Illustration by Paul Wright. 56 ZEFA/B. Simmons. 57 Somerset Levels Project, Devon. 58-59 Illustration by Jim Russell. 59 Photograph Dr Josephine Flood. 60, 61 Peter Kain © Richard Leakey. 63 Illustration by Jim Russell. 64 B. & C. Alexander. 65 Illustration by Terence Dalley. 66-67 B. & C. Alexander. 68 National Museum of Antiquities of Scotland, BL. 68-69, 70 Event Horizons/ David Lyons. 71 Photograph Mick Sharp. 72-73 Illustration by Jim Russell. 73 Photograph E. Callahan, TR. 74 Illustration by Jim Russell. 75 Event Horizons/David Lyons. 76-77 Illustration by Paul Wright. 78 Illustration by Jim Russell. 79 Photograph Dewitt Jones. 80 From Maiden Castle, R.E.M. Wheeler. 81 B. & C. Alexander. 82 Natural History Museum, London. 82 English Heritage Photographic Library. 84-85 Illustration by Sarah Kensington. 86 Photograph Michael Holford. 87 Photograph Michael Holford, T; illustration by Jim Russell, BL. 88 Science Photo Library. 89 Illustrations by Jim Russell, T, BL; National Museum of Antiquities of

Scotland, BM. 90 National Museum, Copenhagen, TL; illustration by David Noonan, BR. 91 Illustrations by David Noonan. 92 Photograph Ira Block. 93 Illustration by Sarah Kensington, TR; TBA, BL. 94 Illustration by Sarah Kensington. 95 Photograph Michael Holford, TL; Devizes Museum, Wiltshire, TR; illustration by Sarah Kensington, BR. 96 Illustration by Sarah Kensington. 97 British Museum, London. 98 Museum of London. 99 AAAC, TL; Newham Museum Service, BR. 100 Science Photo Library. 101 National Museum, Copenhagen. 102 The Department of Antiquities, Israel, Ministry of Education and Culture, BL; AAAC, BM. 102-3 Illustration by Jim Russell. 104 Sonia Halliday Photographs/Jane Taylor. 105 Illustration by Jim Russell. 106 Musée de l'Homme, Collection Henri Lhote/AKG/Eric Lessing. 107 Illustrations by David Noonan/Pitting of Skull, from Osteología Cultural Prácticas Cefálicas, Prof Pedro Weiss; Striated Bone, from Prof Robert A. Benfer, Jr, Department of Anthropology, University of Missouri. 108 Dr Josephine Flood. 109 Silkeborg Museum, Denmark. 110-11 Robert Harding Picture Library/ Adam Woolfitt. 112 Peter Kain © Richard Leakey, BL; illustration by Jim Russell, TR. 113 Peter Kain © Richard Leakey. 114 Kozta Josef-Muzeum/AKG/Eric Lessing, TM; illustration by David Noonan, BL. 115 Sonia Halliday Photographs/Jane Taylor. 116 Illustration by Sarah Kensington. 117 Photograph Mick Sharp. 118 Museo Nacional de Antropología y Arqueología, Lima/Imschoot. 119 Magnum/George Rodger. 120 Illustration by Jim Russell. 121 Robert Harding Picture Library/H.P. Merton. 122-3 Illustration by Terence Dalley. 124 Robert Harding Picture Library/Richard Ashworth. 124-5 Photograph Michael Holford. 126 Illustration by Jim Russell. 127 Iraq Museum, Baghdad/ TBA, TL; TBA, TR; Photograph Michael Holford, BR. 128 AAAC, TL; photograph Michael Holford, BM.

129 Photograph Michael Holford. 130-1 Robert Harding Picture Library. 132 Photograph Johan Reinhard. 133 AAAC. 134 AAAC, TR; illustration by David Noonan, BL. 135 Photograph Michael Holford, TL; Karachi Museum/ Robert Harding Picture Library, BM. 136-7 Illustration by Sarah Kensington. 138 Leningrad State Hermitage Museum. 139 Photograph Michael Holford. 140 Illustration by Sarah Kensington, TM; AKG, B. 141 Illustration by David Noonan. 142 Robert Estall/ David Coulson. 143 Illustration by Sarah Kensington,T; Jericho Excavation Fund, BM. 144-5 Event Horizons/David Lyons. 146 Elizabeth Baquedano, TM, BL. 147 National Museum, Copenhagen, TL; Cambridge University, Museum of Archaeology and Anthropology, BM. 148-9 Event Horizons/David Lyons. 150 E.C. Krupp, from Arqueoastronomía y etnoastronomía en Mesoamérica, J. Broda, Universidad Nacional Autónoma de México. 151 AAAC. 152-3 English Heritage Photographic Library. 154 Illustration by David Noonan, TL; National Geographic Society/Sisse Brimberg, TR; Photograph Michael Holford, MM; Photograph Ira Block, BM. 155 Illustration by David Noonan, TM; Hirmer Archives, ML; Staatliche Museen, Berlin, MR; Robert Harding Picture Library/ Adam Woolfitt, BM.

Front cover: Illustration by Sarah Kensington, TL; Silkeborg Museum, ML; illustration by Jim Russell, MM; Römisch-Germanisches Zentralmuseum, MR; Elizabeth Baquedano, BL; AKG, BM; illustration by David Noonan, BR.

Back cover: B. & C. Alexander, TL; Römisch-Germanisches Zentralmuseum, ML; John Bigelow Taylor, MM; Robert Harding Picture Library/ Photograph H.P. Merton, MR; Robert Harding Picture Library, BL; TBA, BR.